The Complete Flexitarian Cookbook

1800 Days of Delicious, Flexitarian Diet (Flexible Vegetarian) Plant Based Recipes for Part-Time Vegans to Lose Weight and Stay Healthy

Margaret Hann

Table of Contents

Introduction 1

    Understanding the Flexitarian Lifestyle 1

    Benefits of a Flexitarian Diet 1

Chapter 1: Getting Started 3

    Creating a Versatile Pantry for Flexitarian Cooking.............................3

    Essential Kitchen Tools 4

Chapter 2: Flexitarian Basics 5

    The Flexitarian Plate: Finding Balance Between Plant-based and Animal-based Foods..5

    Choosing the Right Protein Sources...6

    Incorporating Whole Grains 6

Chapter 3: Plant-Powered Protein Bowls...7

    Quinoa and Black Bean Fiesta Bowl..7

    Spicy Chickpea and Roasted Vegetable Delight 8

    Lentil and Sweet Potato Harvest Bowl...9

    Edamame and Brown Rice Buddha Bowl 10

    Mexican-Inspired Cauliflower Rice Bowl 11

    Greek-style Hummus and Falafel Bliss 12

    Pesto Zucchini Noodle and White Bean Bowl 14

    Asian-Inspired Tofu and Broccoli Bowl 15

    Southwestern Corn and Avocado Quinoa Bowl 17

    Teriyaki Tempeh and Sesame Seed Sensation 18

    Mediterranean Quinoa and Chickpea Bowl with Tzatziki 19

    Sweet and Spicy Mango Black Rice Bowl with Crispy Tempeh.........21

    Tex-Mex Pinto Bean and Corn Salsa Bowl...22

    Roasted Brussels Sprouts and Pomegranate Quinoa Bowl 24

Thai Basil Coconut Millet Bowl with Crispy Tofu 25

Chapter 4: Flexi-Tacos 27

BBQ Jackfruit Tacos with Slaw 27

Mushroom and Walnut Taco Filling 28

Tofu and Black Bean Tacos with Avocado Lime Crema..........................29

Greek-inspired Chickpea Gyro Tacos 31

Cauliflower and Lentil Lettuce Wrap Tacos 32

Sweet Potato and Black Bean Tacos with Chipotle Crema 34

Teriyaki Portobello Mushroom Tacos..35

Pineapple and Quinoa Stuffed Pepper Tacos 37

Buffalo Cauliflower and Avocado Tacos 39

Jamaican Jerk Cauliflower Tacos with Pineapple Salsa 40

Harissa Spiced Lentil and Cucumber Yogurt Tacos 42

Miso Glazed Eggplant and Avocado Tacos 44

Caprese Style Pesto Quinoa Tacos with Balsamic Reduction 45

Chapter 5: Veggie-Packed Stir-Fries 47

Sesame Ginger Tofu and Broccoli Stir-Fry..47

Coconut Curry Tempeh and Vegetable Stir-Fry 48

Cashew and Vegetable Teriyaki Stir-Fry 49

Peanut Sauce Quinoa and Edamame Stir-Fry 50

Spicy Sriracha Eggplant and Tofu Stir-Fry 52

Orange Glazed Cauliflower and Snap Pea Stir-Fry 53

Thai Basil Tempeh and Bell Pepper Stir-Fry 55

Pineapple Fried Rice with Tofu..56

Lemon Garlic Chickpea and Asparagus Stir-Fry 57

Hoisin Glazed Portobello Mushroom Stir-Fry 58

Mango and Cashew Coconut Rice Stir-Fry..60

Turmeric Roasted Cauliflower and Chickpea Stir-Fry 61

Raspberry Teriyaki Tempeh and Snow Pea Stir-Fry 62

Sesame Orange Glazed Broccoli and Quinoa Stir-Fry..................................64

Chapter 6: Protein-Packed Pastas..................................66

Lentil and Spinach Stuffed Shells 66

Chickpea and Artichoke Linguine 67

Pesto Zoodle Primavera..................................68

Walnut and Mushroom Bolognese Spaghetti..................................70

Roasted Red Pepper and White Bean Penne 71

Spinach and Ricotta Stuffed Manicotti 72

Lemon Garlic Edamame and Cherry Tomato Linguine 74

Cilantro Lime Black Bean and Corn Fusilli 75

Butternut Squash and Sage Farfalle 76

Tomato Basil Quinoa Mac 'n' Cheese 77

Spinach and Artichoke Stuffed Shells with Walnut Parmesan 79

Sundried Tomato and Basil Chickpea Penne 80

Lemon Dijon Asparagus and White Bean Linguine 81

Butternut Squash and Sage Gnocchi with Almond Cream Sauce..................................83

Pesto Zoodle Caprese Salad with Balsamic Drizzle 84

Chapter 7: Seafood Alternatives..................................87

Almond Crusted Tofu "Fish" and Chips 87

Seared Tempeh "Scallops" with Lemon Butter Sauce..................................88

Cajun Spiced Chickpea Cakes with Remoulade 89

Teriyaki Glazed Eggplant "Eel" Sushi Bowl 91

Artichoke and Hearts of Palm "Crab" Cakes 92

Lemon Dill Quinoa Stuffed Bell Peppers with "Shrimp" 93

Coconut-Curry Seitan "Shrimp" Stir-Fry 94

Blackened Jackfruit "Tuna" Salad Wraps 96

Mediterranean Stuffed Zucchini with "Feta" and "Shrimp" 97

Spicy Mango Glazed Jackfruit "Shrimp" Lettuce Wraps 98

Smoked Paprika Seitan "Scallops" with Garlic Aioli 100

Lemon Herb Grilled Tofu "Fish" Tacos...101

Coconut Curry Cauliflower "Crab" Soup 102

Crispy Teriyaki Tempeh "Tuna" Poke Bowl 103

Chapter 8: Grain-Free Delights...106

Spaghetti Squash Pad Thai with Tofu 106

Cauliflower and Chickpea Crust Pizza..107

Zucchini Lasagna with Cashew Ricotta 109

Portobello Mushroom Cap Burgers with Guacamole 110

Eggplant Rollatini with Vegan Pesto 112

Quinoa and Black Bean Stuffed Bell Peppers................................114

Sweet Potato and Lentil Patties with Avocado Aioli 115

Coconut Curry Butternut Squash Soup with Quinoa 116

Spaghetti Squash Alfredo with Broccoli and Sun-Dried Tomatoes.................118

Portobello Mushroom and Spinach Enchilada Stacks.....................119

Sweet Potato and Chickpea Patties with Cilantro Lime Sauce 120

Eggplant and Zucchini Noodle Caprese Salad................................121

Chapter 9: 30-Day Meal Plan 123

Week 1: 123

Week 2: 124

Week 3: 125

Week 4: 125

Chapter 10: Dining Out as a Flexitarian 128

Exploring Menu Options 128

Making Smart Dining Choices 128

Chapter 11: Maintaining a Healthy and Balanced Flexitarian Lifestyle 130

Tips for Long-term Success..130

Chapter 12: Flexitarian Terms Glossary...............................132

Conclusion..134

Index of Recipes 135

Introduction

Step into the world of flexible and delectable dining with *The Complete Flexitarian Cookbook*! This cookbook is a comprehensive guide that effortlessly blends the finest elements of plant-based and animal-based lifestyles. Whether you're an experienced flexitarian or new to this delicious culinary adventure, these pages are packed with recipes and insights to ensure a seamless and flavorful transition.

Understanding the Flexitarian Lifestyle

The term "flexitarian" is a combination of "flexible" and "vegetarian," highlighting the flexible and inclusive nature of this dietary approach. The flexitarian lifestyle promotes a diet that is primarily focused on plant-based foods, with the flexibility to include meat and other animal products on occasion. It's not about following rigid guidelines or restrictions, but rather about making thoughtful and adaptable decisions that reflect your personal preferences, health objectives, and ethical values.

Flexitarians prioritize a diet that includes a variety of fruits, vegetables, whole grains, legumes, and nuts, while also allowing for occasional consumption of lean meats, poultry, fish, and dairy foods. This approach offers a wide range of benefits that address both individual health and environmental concerns.

Benefits of a Flexitarian Diet

1. Nutrient Diversity: By including a wide array of plant-based foods, flexitarians naturally boost their nutrient intake, acquiring a variety of essential vitamins, minerals, and antioxidants that are essential to maintaining good health.

2. Weight Management: The flexitarian diet is recognized for its ability to support weight management and encourage a healthy body composition. The focus on plant-based foods typically results in a reduction in calorie consumption and a greater feeling of satiety.

3. Heart Health: The flexitarian diet prioritizes plant-derived foods, which has been linked to improved heart health, including lower cholesterol levels and a decreased risk of heart disease. The incorporation of heart-healthy fats from sources such as avocados and nuts additionally enhances cardiovascular health.

4. Sustainability: Embracing a flexitarian lifestyle can have a positive impact on the environment. By reducing dependency on animal products, adopters can make a positive impact on greenhouse gas emissions and promote a more sustainable food production system.

5. Flexibility and Delight: Embrace flexibility and find joy in your eating habits with the flexitarian approach. There's provision to enjoy your favorite meals, treat yourself occasionally, and find excitement in exploring new plant-based recipes.

As you explore the pages of this cookbook, you'll find a wide range of recipes that emphasize the delicious flavors and nutritional benefits of the flexitarian lifestyle. If you're looking to improve your eating habits, discover more plant-based options, or uncover new culinary ideas, this cookbook will be your guide to a healthier and more enjoyable approach to food. Let's embark on this delightful journey together!

Chapter 1: Getting Started

Starting your flexitarian journey is an exhilarating move towards a more conscious and well-rounded approach to eating. In this chapter, we'll provide you with a comprehensive guide to help you begin your journey into the flexitarian lifestyle. We'll also offer valuable tips on how to set up your kitchen for optimal success. By ensuring you have a well-stocked pantry and the necessary kitchen tools, we can help you lay the groundwork for preparing tasty and healthy flexitarian meals.

Creating a Versatile Pantry for Flexitarian Cooking

A well-stocked pantry is essential for easy and diverse flexitarian cooking. With a variety of versatile ingredients at your disposal, you'll be able to effortlessly create mouthwatering meals in no time. Here's a guide to help you establish a well-stocked flexitarian pantry:

1. Whole Grains: Make sure to stock up your pantry with a diverse selection of whole grains such as quinoa, brown rice, farro, and oats. These grains are an excellent base for a variety of flexitarian meals, offering essential fiber and nutrients.

2. Legumes and Pulses: Make sure to have a good supply of canned or dried legumes like lentils, chickpeas, black beans, and kidney beans. These plant-based protein sources bring a hearty and nutritious boost to salads, soups, and stews.

3. Nuts and Seeds: Always have a variety of nuts (almonds, walnuts, cashews) and seeds (chia, flax, pumpkin) on hand to enhance texture, flavor, and provide a balanced supply of healthy fats. They're ideal for adding to salads, yogurt, or blending into smoothies.

4. Healthy Oils: Choose heart-healthy oils such as olive oil, avocado oil, and coconut oil. These are crucial for cooking and dressing salads, offering necessary fatty acids and rich flavors.

5. Herbs and Spices: Enhance the flavor of your dishes by incorporating a wide variety of herbs and spices, allowing you to reduce your reliance on excessive salt or sugar. Essentials consist of garlic, onion powder, cumin, paprika, and a selection of dried herbs.

6. Plant-Based Proteins: Explore the wide range of plant-based protein options available, including tofu, tempeh, and plant-based meat alternatives. These versatile ingredients can be used in a variety of flexitarian recipes, ranging from stir-fries to tacos.

7. Canned Tomatoes and Sauces: Stock up on a variety of canned tomatoes, tomato paste, and sauces such as soy sauce and hot sauce. These ingredients will enhance the taste and richness of your meals.

8. Whole Fruits and Vegetables: Although fresh fruits and vegetables are essential, having a stock of canned or frozen fruits and vegetables is a great way to ensure a constant supply of nutritious options, even when fresh produce is not readily available.

Essential Kitchen Tools

Having the proper tools in your kitchen can greatly enhance your flexitarian cooking experience, making it more pleasurable and efficient. Presenting a comprehensive list of indispensable kitchen tools to support your flexitarian journey:

1. High-Quality Knives: Consider investing in a set of top-notch knives that are sharp and reliable for all your chopping, dicing, and slicing needs when working with fruits, vegetables, and proteins.

2. Cutting Board: Get a cutting board that is durable and provides a safe and clean surface for food preparation.

3. Blender or Food Processor: These incredibly versatile appliances are perfect for creating a wide range of delicious recipes, from refreshing smoothies and flavorful sauces to creamy dips and even homemade nut butters.

4. Non-Stick Skillet: A non-stick skillet is perfect for sautéing vegetables and cooking plant-based proteins with very little oil.

5. Baking Sheets: Baking sheets are a must-have for roasting vegetables, making sheet pan meals, and baking delicious treats.

6. Measuring Cups and Spoons: Precise measurements are essential in cooking, particularly when trying out new recipes. Measuring cups and spoons help you to control portions when making dishes.

7. Vegetable Peeler: A reliable vegetable peeler efficiently peels and prepares a broad range of vegetables.

8. Mixing Bowls: Make sure to have a range of mixing bowls available in various sizes for effortlessly combining ingredients and creating delicious salads.

9. Sieve or Colander: These tools are useful for draining and rinsing canned beans, grains, and pasta.

10. Storage Containers: Consider purchasing a variety of airtight containers to help keep your leftovers and meal prepped ingredients fresh.

With a well-stocked flexitarian pantry and the right kitchen tools, you'll be fully equipped to delve into the delicious and diverse realm of flexitarian cooking.

Chapter 2: Flexitarian Basics

In this Flexitarian Basics chapter, we'll explore the fundamental principles of the flexitarian lifestyle, providing guidance on how to create a balanced and nutritious plate that embraces the benefits of both plant-based and animal-based foods. Having a solid grasp of the fundamentals of the Flexitarian Plate, making smart protein selections, and including whole grains are essential components that will enable you to craft delectable and nourishing meals that support your flexitarian objectives.

The Flexitarian Plate: Finding Balance Between Plant-based and Animal-based Foods

The core principle of the flexitarian lifestyle is centered around finding a harmonious balance. The Flexitarian Plate is a helpful tool that promotes a balanced and nutritious meal by suggesting a mindful combination of plant-based and animal-based foods. Here's1 a breakdown of the Flexitarian Plate:

• Vegetables and Fruits (50%): Make sure to include a colorful variety of vegetables and fruits on half of your plate. These nutrient-rich choices offer vital vitamins, minerals, and antioxidants, promoting overall health and well-being.

• Plant-Based Proteins (25%): Dedicate a quarter of your plate to plant-based protein sources like legumes, tofu, tempeh, and plant-based meat alternatives. These options provide a good amount of protein and also offer important fiber and other nutrients.

• Animal-Based Proteins (25%): Allocate the remaining quarter of your plate for lean and sustainable animal-based proteins. Choose sources such as poultry, fish, and lean cuts of meat to ensure you're getting the necessary amino acids and micronutrients.

• Whole Grains or Starchy Vegetables (Optional): You may choose to include a small portion of whole grains or starchy vegetables on the side if you'd like. Consider incorporating brown rice, quinoa, sweet potatoes, or whole-grain pasta into your meals to enhance feelings of fullness and boost your energy levels.

This flexible approach enables you to customize the proportions according to your preferences and nutritional requirements, offering a visual tool to assist you in meal planning and guaranteeing a balanced and enjoyable dining experience.

Choosing the Right Protein Sources

Protein plays a crucial role in the flexitarian diet, and by making wise choices, you can meet your nutritional requirements while maintaining a well-rounded lifestyle. These protein choices are ideal for flexitarians:

- **Legumes:** Include a diverse selection of legumes like lentils, chickpeas, black beans, and edamame in your meals. These plant-based powerhouses are packed with protein, fiber, and essential nutrients.
- **Tofu and Tempeh:** Tap into the incredible versatility of tofu and tempeh, two fantastic options for plant-based protein. They have a remarkable ability to absorb flavors, making them an excellent choice for a variety of savory and sweet dishes.
- **Nuts and Seeds:** Incorporate a variety of nuts and seeds such as almonds, walnuts, chia seeds, and hemp seeds into your meals to enhance protein content, provide healthy fats, and add texture.
- **Fish and Seafood:** Choose fatty fish such as salmon, which offers omega-3 fatty acids and protein. Seafood, overall, is a healthy and nutritious choice.
- **Poultry and Lean Meats:** Opt for lean cuts of poultry like chicken or turkey, as well as lean cuts of red meat. These animal-based proteins provide crucial amino acids and valuable nutrients.

Incorporating Whole Grains

Whole grains are an essential part of the flexitarian diet, providing a wealth of complex carbohydrates, fiber, and a variety of nutrients. Here's a simple way to include whole grains in your flexitarian meals:

- **Quinoa:** Quinoa is a highly versatile and protein-rich grain that can be used as a base for salads, bowls, or as a side dish.
- **Brown Rice:** Consider replacing white rice with brown rice for a boost in fiber and essential nutrients.
- **Whole Wheat Pasta:** Opt for whole wheat pasta to add more heartiness and nutrients to your favorite pasta dishes.
- **Farro and Barley:** Try incorporating time-tested grains like farro and barley into your salads and stews for a delightful chewy texture and rich nutty flavor.
- **Oats:** Begin your mornings with a nourishing and fulfilling breakfast of oatmeal, garnished with fresh fruits and nuts.

As you explore this cookbook further, you'll find a wide range of recipes that embody these principles, providing a variety of delicious dishes for all taste preferences and occasions. Prepare yourself for a delightful experience that combines the best aspects of both worlds during your flexitarian journey!

Chapter 3: Plant-Powered Protein Bowls

Quinoa and Black Bean Fiesta Bowl

Prep Time: 15 minutes
Cook Time: 25 minutes
Servings: 4

Ingredients:

- 1 cup quinoa (rinsed and drained)
- 2 cups vegetable broth
- 1 can (15 ounces) black beans (drained and rinsed)
- 1 cup corn kernels (fresh or frozen)
- 1 cup cherry tomatoes (halved)
- 1 avocado (diced)
- ½ red onion (finely chopped)
- ¼ cup fresh cilantro (chopped)
- 1 lime (juiced)
- 1 teaspoon ground cumin
- 1 teaspoon chili powder
- Salt and pepper to taste

Directions:

1. In a medium saucepan, add in the quinoa and vegetable broth.
2. Bring to a boil, then reduce heat to low, cover, and simmer for 15 minutes or until quinoa is cooked and liquid is absorbed.
3. While quinoa is cooking, in a separate pan, heat black beans over medium heat until warmed through.
4. If using fresh corn, heat a skillet over medium-high heat.
5. Add corn kernels and cook until they start to char, about 5 minutes. If using frozen corn, simply thaw.
6. In serving bowls, add in the cooked quinoa, black beans, roasted corn, cherry tomatoes, diced avocado, red onion, and chopped cilantro, and stir to combine.
7. In a small bowl, mix lime juice, ground cumin, chili powder, salt, and pepper.
8. Drizzle the seasoning over the bowl and toss gently to combine.
9. Divide the mixture among the serving bowls.

Nutritional Information (Per Serving):

- **Carbs:** 57g

- **Fats:** 15g

- **Fiber:** 15g

- **Protein:** 15g

Spicy Chickpea and Roasted Vegetable Delight

Prep Time: 20 minutes
Cook Time: 30 minutes
Servings: 4

Ingredients:

- 2 cans (15 ounces each) chickpeas (drained and rinsed)

- 1 large sweet potato (peeled and diced)

- 2 bell peppers (sliced)

- 1 zucchini (sliced)

- 1 red onion (cut into wedges)

- 3 tablespoons olive oil

- 1 teaspoon cumin

- 1 teaspoon smoked paprika

- ½ teaspoon cayenne pepper

- Salt and pepper to taste

- 1 cup cherry tomatoes (halved)

- 2 cups baby spinach

- ¼ cup feta cheese (crumbled, optional)

Directions:

1. Preheat the oven to 425°F (220°C).
2. In a large bowl, add in the chickpeas, diced sweet potato, sliced bell peppers, sliced zucchini, and red onion wedges.
3. Drizzle with olive oil and toss to coat.
4. Sprinkle cumin, smoked paprika, cayenne pepper, salt, and pepper over the vegetables, tossing again to evenly distribute the spices.

5. Spread the seasoned vegetables on a baking sheet in a single layer.
6. Roast in the preheated oven for 25-30 minutes or until the vegetables are tender and slightly crispy.
7. In the last 5 minutes of roasting, add halved cherry tomatoes to the baking sheet.
8. In a large serving bowl, place baby spinach.
9. Once roasted, transfer the vegetables and chickpeas to the bowl with spinach, allowing the heat to slightly wilt the spinach.
10. Toss everything together until properly combined.
11. If desired, sprinkle crumbled feta cheese on top.

Nutritional Information (Per Serving):

- **Carbs:** 45g

- **Fats:** 12g

- **Fiber:** 12g

- **Protein:** 13g

Lentil and Sweet Potato Harvest Bowl

Prep Time: 15 minutes
Cook Time: 25 minutes
Servings: 4

Ingredients:

- 1 cup dried green lentils

- 2 large sweet potatoes (peeled and diced)

- 1 red onion (sliced)

- 2 tablespoons olive oil

- 1 teaspoon ground cumin

- 1 teaspoon ground coriander

- ½ teaspoon cinnamon

- Salt and pepper to taste

- 2 cups Brussels sprouts (trimmed and halved)

- 1 cup pomegranate arils

- ½ cup crumbled goat cheese (optional)

- ¼ cup chopped fresh parsley

Directions:

1. Rinse the dried green lentils and cook according to package instructions. Set aside.
2. Preheat the oven to 425°F (220°C).
3. On a baking sheet, toss diced sweet potatoes and sliced red onion with olive oil, ground cumin, ground coriander, cinnamon, salt, and pepper.
4. Roast for 20-25 minutes or until sweet potatoes are tender.
5. In the last 10 minutes of roasting, add halved Brussels sprouts to the baking sheet, tossing to coat in the seasoned oil.
6. In serving bowls, add in the cooked lentils, roasted sweet potatoes, red onion, and Brussels sprouts, and stir to combine.
7. Top the bowl with pomegranate arils and crumbled goat cheese (if using).
8. Sprinkle chopped fresh parsley over the bowl.

Nutritional Information (Per Serving):

- **Carbs:** 58g

- **Fats:** 8g

- **Fiber:** 17g

- **Protein:** 18g

Edamame and Brown Rice Buddha Bowl

Prep Time: 15 minutes
Cook Time: 45 minutes (includes rice cooking time)
Servings: 4

Ingredients:

- 1 cup brown rice (uncooked)

- 2 cups edamame (shelled)

- 2 carrots (julienned)

- 1 red bell pepper (sliced)

- 1 cucumber (sliced)

- 1 avocado (sliced)

- 4 green onions (sliced)

- ¼ cup soy sauce

- 2 tablespoons sesame oil

- 1 tablespoon rice vinegar

- 1 tablespoon maple syrup

- 1 teaspoon grated ginger

- 1 clove garlic (minced)

- Sesame seeds for garnish

Directions:

1. Cook brown rice according to package instructions. Set aside.
2. Steam or boil shelled edamame until tender, then drain.
3. Julienne carrots, slice red bell pepper, cucumber, avocado, and green onions.
4. In serving bowls, arrange cooked brown rice, steamed edamame, julienned carrots, sliced red bell pepper, cucumber, avocado, and green onions.
5. In a small bowl, whisk together soy sauce, sesame oil, rice vinegar, maple syrup, grated ginger, and minced garlic.
6. Drizzle the dressing over the Buddha bowl.
7. Sprinkle sesame seeds on top as garnish.
8. Serve immediately.

Nutritional Information (Per Serving):

- **Carbs:** 58g

- **Fats:** 18g

- **Fiber:** 14g

- **Protein:** 22g

Mexican-Inspired Cauliflower Rice Bowl

Prep Time: 20 minutes
Cook Time: 15 minutes
Servings: 4

Ingredients:

- 1 large head cauliflower (riced)

- 1 tablespoon olive oil

- 1 onion (diced)

- 2 bell peppers (diced)

- 1 cup black beans (canned, drained, and rinsed)

- 1 cup corn kernels (fresh or frozen)

- 1 teaspoon ground cumin

- 1 teaspoon chili powder

- ½ teaspoon smoked paprika

- Salt and pepper to taste

- 1 avocado (sliced)

- 1 cup cherry tomatoes (halved)

- ¼ cup fresh cilantro (chopped)

- Lime wedges for serving

Directions:

1. Cut the cauliflower into florets and place them in a food processor.
2. Pulse until cauliflower resembles rice. Set aside.
3. In a large skillet, heat olive oil over medium heat.
4. Add diced onion and sauté until translucent.
5. Add diced bell peppers and continue to sauté until the vegetables are tender.
6. Push the sautéed vegetables to one side of the skillet and add the riced cauliflower to the empty side.
7. Sprinkle ground cumin, chili powder, smoked paprika, salt, and pepper over the cauliflower rice.
8. Stir to combine and cook for 5-7 minutes until the cauliflower is tender.
9. Incorporate black beans and corn into the cauliflower rice mixture.
10. Cook for an additional 2-3 minutes until everything is heated through.
11. Divide the cauliflower rice mixture among serving bowls.
12. Top each bowl with sliced avocado, halved cherry tomatoes, and chopped cilantro.
13. Serve with lime wedges on the side.

Nutritional Information (Per Serving):

- **Carbs:** 45g

- **Fats:** 12g

- **Fiber:** 15g

- **Protein:** 14g

Greek-style Hummus and Falafel Bliss

Prep Time: 30 minutes
Cook Time: 15 minutes
Servings: 4

Ingredients:

For the Falafel:

- 1 can (15 ounces) chickpeas (drained and rinsed)
- ½ cup fresh parsley (chopped)
- ¼ cup red onion (finely diced)
- 2 cloves garlic (minced)
- 1 teaspoon ground cumin
- 1 teaspoon ground coriander
- ½ teaspoon baking powder
- Salt and pepper to taste
- Olive oil for frying

For the Hummus:

- 1 can (15 ounces) chickpeas (drained and rinsed)
- ¼ cup tahini
- 2 tablespoons olive oil
- 1 clove garlic (minced)
- 1 lemon (juiced)
- Salt to taste
- Water (as needed for consistency)

For Serving:

- Pita bread or flatbread
- 1 cucumber (sliced)
- 1 tomato (diced)
- Red onion (sliced)
- Kalamata olives
- Feta cheese (crumbled)
- Fresh mint leaves

Directions:

Falafel:

1. In a food processor, add in the chickpeas, chopped parsley, diced red onion, minced garlic, ground cumin, ground coriander, baking powder, salt, and pepper.
2. Process until the mixture comes together but still has some texture.
3. Shape the mixture into small patties.
4. Heat olive oil in a pan over medium heat.
5. Fry the falafel patties until golden brown on both sides. Place on a paper towel to absorb excess oil.
6. In a blender or food processor, blend chickpeas, tahini, olive oil, minced garlic, lemon juice, and salt until smooth.
7. Add water as needed to achieve the desired consistency.
8. Warm the pita bread or flatbread.
9. Arrange sliced cucumber, diced tomato, sliced red onion, Kalamata olives, and crumbled feta cheese.
10. Spread a generous amount of hummus on each plate.
11. Place falafel patties on top of the hummus.
12. Arrange the prepared serving ingredients around the falafel and hummus.
13. Garnish with fresh mint leaves.

Nutritional Information (Per Serving):

- **Carbs:** 60g
- **Fats:** 20g
- **Fiber:** 15g
- **Protein:** 18g

Pesto Zucchini Noodle and White Bean Bowl

Prep Time: 20 minutes
Cook Time: 10 minutes
Servings: 4

Ingredients:

- 4 medium zucchinis (spiralized into noodles)
- 2 tablespoons olive oil
- 2 cloves garlic (minced)
- 1 can (15 ounces) white beans (cannellini or any preferred type, drained and rinsed)
- 1 cup cherry tomatoes (halved)
- ½ cup pesto sauce

- Salt and pepper to taste

- Grated Parmesan cheese for topping (optional)

- Fresh basil leaves for garnish

Directions:

1. Spiralize the zucchinis into noodle shapes. Set aside.
2. In a large pan, heat olive oil over medium heat.
3. Add minced garlic and sauté for about 1 minute until fragrant.
4. Add zucchini noodles and sauté for 2-3 minutes until they are just tender. Avoid overcooking.
5. Incorporate drained and rinsed white beans into the pan with zucchini noodles.
6. Add halved cherry tomatoes and cook for an additional 2-3 minutes until heated through.
7. Stir in the pesto sauce, ensuring that the zucchini noodles, white beans, and tomatoes are well coated.
8. Season with salt and pepper to taste.
9. Divide the mixture into serving bowls.
10. Optionally, top with grated Parmesan cheese.
11. Garnish with fresh basil leaves.

Nutritional Information (Per Serving):

- **Carbs:** 40g

- **Fats:** 18g

- **Fiber:** 10g

- **Protein:** 14g

Asian-Inspired Tofu and Broccoli Bowl

Prep Time: 30 minutes
Cook Time: 20 minutes
Servings: 4

Ingredients:

For the Tofu:

- 1 block (14 ounces) extra-firm tofu (pressed and cubed)

- 2 tablespoons soy sauce

- 1 tablespoon sesame oil

- 1 tablespoon cornstarch

- 1 teaspoon garlic powder
- 1 teaspoon ginger (minced)

For the Stir-Fry:

- 2 tablespoons vegetable oil
- 1 broccoli head (cut into florets)
- 1 bell pepper (sliced)
- 1 carrot (julienned)
- 3 green onions (sliced)
- 2 cloves garlic (minced)
- ¼ cup soy sauce
- 2 tablespoons hoisin sauce
- 1 tablespoon rice vinegar
- 1 tablespoon brown sugar
- 1 teaspoon sesame oil
- Sesame seeds for garnish

For Serving:

- Cooked brown rice or quinoa

Directions:

1. Press the tofu to remove excess water, then cut it into cubes.
2. In a bowl, mix soy sauce, sesame oil, cornstarch, garlic powder, and minced ginger.
3. Toss the tofu cubes in the marinade and let it sit for at least 15 minutes.
4. Heat a large skillet over medium-high heat.
5. Add marinated tofu cubes and cook until all sides are golden brown. Set aside.
6. In the same skillet, add vegetable oil.
7. Sauté broccoli florets, sliced bell pepper, julienned carrot, sliced green onions, and minced garlic until vegetables are tender-crisp.
8. In a small bowl, whisk together soy sauce, hoisin sauce, rice vinegar, brown sugar, and sesame oil.
9. Add the cooked tofu back to the skillet with sautéed vegetables.
10. Pour the prepared sauce over the tofu and vegetables.
11. Toss everything together until well coated and heated through.
12. Serve the tofu and vegetable stir-fry over cooked brown rice or quinoa.

- Garnish with sesame seeds before serving.

Nutritional Information (Per Serving):

- **Carbs:** 40g

- **Fats:** 18g

- **Fiber:** 8g

- **Protein:** 20g

Southwestern Corn and Avocado Quinoa Bowl

Prep Time: 20 minutes
Cook Time: 15 minutes
Servings: 4

Ingredients:

- 1 cup quinoa (rinsed and drained)

- 2 cups vegetable broth

- 1 can (15 ounces) black beans (drained and rinsed)

- 1 cup corn kernels (fresh or frozen)

- 1 red bell pepper (diced)

- 1 avocado (diced)

- ½ red onion (finely chopped)

- ¼ cup fresh cilantro (chopped)

- 1 lime (juiced)

- 1 teaspoon ground cumin

- 1 teaspoon chili powder

- Salt and pepper to taste

Directions:

1. In a medium saucepan, add in the quinoa and vegetable broth.
2. Bring to a boil, then reduce heat to low, cover, and simmer for 15 minutes or until quinoa is cooked and liquid is absorbed.
3. While quinoa is cooking, in a separate pan, heat black beans over medium heat until warmed through.
4. If using fresh corn, heat a skillet over medium-high heat.

5. Add corn kernels and cook until they start to char, about 5 minutes. If using frozen corn, simply thaw.
6. In serving bowls, add in the cooked quinoa, black beans, roasted corn, diced red bell pepper, diced avocado, finely chopped red onion, and chopped cilantro, and stir to combine.
7. In a small bowl, mix lime juice, ground cumin, chili powder, salt, and pepper.
8. Drizzle the seasoning over the bowl and toss gently to combine.
9. Divide the mixture among the serving bowls.

Nutritional Information (Per Serving):

- **Carbs:** 60g

- **Fats:** 15g

- **Fiber:** 15g

- **Protein:** 16g

Teriyaki Tempeh and Sesame Seed Sensation

Prep Time: 25 minutes
Cook Time: 15 minutes
Servings: 4

Ingredients:

- 2 packages (8 ounces each) tempeh (sliced into cubes)

- 1 cup low-sodium soy sauce

- ¼ cup mirin

- 2 tablespoons rice vinegar

- 2 tablespoons maple syrup

- 1 teaspoon sesame oil

- 1 teaspoon ginger (minced)

- 2 cloves garlic (minced)

- 2 tablespoons vegetable oil

- 1 tablespoon cornstarch

- 2 tablespoons water

- 2 tablespoons sesame seeds (toasted)

- Green onions for garnish (sliced)
- Cooked brown rice for serving

Directions:

1. In a bowl, whisk together soy sauce, mirin, rice vinegar, maple syrup, sesame oil, minced ginger, and minced garlic.
2. Place tempeh cubes in the marinade and let it marinate for at least 15 minutes.
3. In a large skillet, heat vegetable oil over medium-high heat.
4. Add marinated tempeh cubes and sear until golden brown on all sides.
5. In a small bowl, mix cornstarch with water to create a slurry.
6. Add the slurry to the remaining marinade to thicken it into a teriyaki sauce.
7. Pour the teriyaki sauce over the seared tempeh in the skillet.
8. Continue cooking until the teriyaki sauce coats the tempeh and thickens.
9. Serve the teriyaki tempeh over cooked brown rice.
10. Garnish with toasted sesame seeds and sliced green onions.

Nutritional Information (Per Serving):

- **Carbs:** 40g
- **Fats:** 18g
- **Fiber:** 8g
- **Protein:** 24g

Mediterranean Quinoa and Chickpea Bowl with Tzatziki

Prep Time: 20 minutes
Cook Time: 15 minutes
Servings: 4

Ingredients:

For the Quinoa and Chickpea Bowl:

- 1 cup quinoa (rinsed and drained)
- 2 cups vegetable broth
- 1 can (15 ounces) chickpeas (drained and rinsed)
- 1 cup cherry tomatoes (halved)
- 1 cucumber (diced)
- ½ red onion (finely chopped)
- ¼ cup Kalamata olives (pitted and sliced)

- ¼ cup fresh parsley (chopped)
- ¼ cup feta cheese (crumbled, optional)
- 2 tablespoons extra-virgin olive oil
- 1 lemon (juiced)
- Salt and pepper to taste

For the Tzatziki:

- 1 cup Greek yogurt
- 1 cucumber (seeded and finely diced)
- 2 cloves garlic (minced)
- 1 tablespoon fresh dill (chopped)
- 1 tablespoon extra-virgin olive oil
- Salt and pepper to taste

Directions:

1. In a medium saucepan, add in the quinoa and vegetable broth.
2. Bring to a boil, then reduce heat to low, cover, and simmer for 15 minutes or until quinoa is cooked and liquid is absorbed.
3. While quinoa is cooking, in a separate pan, heat chickpeas over medium heat until warmed through.
4. In serving bowls, add in the cooked quinoa, warmed chickpeas, halved cherry tomatoes, diced cucumber, finely chopped red onion, sliced Kalamata olives, and chopped fresh parsley, and stir to combine.
5. Drizzle extra-virgin olive oil and lemon juice over the bowl.
6. Season with salt and pepper to taste.
7. If desired, sprinkle crumbled feta cheese on top.
8. In a bowl, add in the Greek yogurt, finely diced cucumber, minced garlic, chopped fresh dill, and extra-virgin olive oil, and stir to combine.
9. Season with salt and pepper to taste.

Serve:

6. **Serve with Tzatziki:**

   - Serve the quinoa and chickpea bowl with a generous dollop of tzatziki on top.

Nutritional Information (Per Serving):

- **Carbs:** 55g
- **Fats:** 18g

- **Fiber:** 11g

- **Protein:** 16g

Sweet and Spicy Mango Black Rice Bowl with Crispy Tempeh

Prep Time: 30 minutes
Cook Time: 30 minutes
Servings: 4

Ingredients:

For the Black Rice Bowl:

- 1 cup black rice

- 2 cups water

- 2 large mangoes (peeled and diced)

- 1 red bell pepper (diced)

- ½ red onion (finely chopped)

- 1 cup snap peas (sliced)

- ¼ cup fresh cilantro (chopped)

- 1 tablespoon sesame seeds (toasted, for garnish)

- 1 tablespoon olive oil

- Salt to taste

For the Crispy Tempeh:

- 2 packages (8 ounces each) tempeh (sliced into cubes)

- 2 tablespoons soy sauce

- 1 tablespoon maple syrup

- 1 tablespoon Sriracha sauce

- 1 tablespoon cornstarch

- 2 tablespoons vegetable oil

For the Sweet and Spicy Mango Sauce:

- 1 large mango (peeled and diced)

- ¼ cup rice vinegar

- 2 tablespoons soy sauce

- 1 tablespoon maple syrup

- 1 tablespoon Sriracha sauce

- 1 clove garlic (minced)

- 1 teaspoon grated ginger

Directions:

1. In a saucepan, add in the black rice and water.
2. Bring to a boil, then reduce heat, cover, and simmer for 30 minutes or until rice is tender and water is absorbed.
3. In a large bowl, add in the diced mangoes, diced red bell pepper, finely chopped red onion, sliced snap peas, and chopped cilantro.
4. Once black rice is cooked, fluff it with a fork and add it to the bowl with the prepared vegetables.
5. Drizzle olive oil over the mixture and season with salt to taste.
6. Toss everything together gently.
7. In a bowl, add in the tempeh cubes with soy sauce, maple syrup, Sriracha sauce, and cornstarch, and stir to combine. Let it marinate for at least 15 minutes.
8. In a skillet, heat vegetable oil over medium-high heat.
9. Add marinated tempeh cubes and cook until crispy on all sides.
10. In a blender, add in the diced mango, rice vinegar, soy sauce, maple syrup, Sriracha sauce, minced garlic, and grated ginger.
11. Blend until smooth.
12. Divide the black rice and vegetable mixture among serving bowls.
13. Top with crispy tempeh cubes.
14. Drizzle the sweet and spicy mango sauce over the bowls.
15. Garnish with toasted sesame seeds.

Nutritional Information (Per Serving):

- **Carbs:** 60g

- **Fats:** 18g

- **Fiber:** 10g

- **Protein:** 20g

Tex-Mex Pinto Bean and Corn Salsa Bowl

Prep Time: 20 minutes
Cook Time: 10 minutes
Servings: 4

Ingredients:

- 2 cups cooked brown rice
- 1 can (15 ounces) pinto beans (canned, drained, and rinsed)
- 1 cup corn kernels (fresh or frozen, thawed)
- 1 red bell pepper (diced)
- 1 avocado (diced)
- ½ red onion (finely chopped)
- 1 jalapeño (seeded and minced)
- ¼ cup fresh cilantro (chopped)
- Juice of 2 limes
- 2 tablespoons olive oil
- 1 teaspoon ground cumin
- 1 teaspoon chili powder
- Salt and pepper to taste
- ¼ cup shredded cheddar cheese (optional, for topping)
- Sour cream or Greek yogurt for serving (optional)

Directions:

1. Cook brown rice according to package instructions.
2. In a saucepan, heat the pinto beans over medium heat until warmed through.
3. In a large bowl, add in the corn kernels, diced red bell pepper, diced avocado, finely chopped red onion, seeded and minced jalapeño, and chopped cilantro.
4. In a small bowl, whisk together lime juice, olive oil, ground cumin, chili powder, salt, and pepper.
5. Divide the cooked brown rice among serving bowls.
6. Top with warmed pinto beans and the corn salsa mixture.
7. Drizzle the dressing over the bowls.
8. Optionally, top with shredded cheddar cheese.
9. Serve with a dollop of sour cream or Greek yogurt if desired.

Nutritional Information (Per Serving):

- **Carbs:** 55g
- **Fats:** 15g
- **Fiber:** 14g

- **Protein:** 12g

Roasted Brussels Sprouts and Pomegranate Quinoa Bowl

Prep Time: 20 minutes
Cook Time: 25 minutes
Servings: 4

Ingredients:

- 1 cup quinoa (rinsed and drained)
- 2 cups vegetable broth
- 1 pound Brussels sprouts (trimmed and halved)
- 2 tablespoons olive oil
- Salt and pepper to taste
- 1 cup pomegranate arils
- ½ cup feta cheese (crumbled, optional)
- ¼ cup pumpkin seeds (toasted)
- Balsamic glaze for drizzling

Directions:

1. In a medium saucepan, add in the quinoa and vegetable broth.
2. Bring to a boil, then reduce heat to low, cover, and simmer for 15 minutes or until quinoa is cooked and liquid is absorbed.
3. Preheat the oven to 400°F (200°C).
4. On a baking sheet, toss halved Brussels sprouts with olive oil, salt, and pepper.
5. Roast in the preheated oven for 20-25 minutes or until Brussels sprouts are golden brown and crispy on the edges.
6. While the quinoa and Brussels sprouts are cooking, toast pumpkin seeds in a dry skillet until they start to pop.
7. If using, crumble the feta cheese.
8. Fluff the cooked quinoa with a fork and divide it among serving bowls.
9. Arrange the roasted Brussels sprouts on top of the quinoa in each bowl.
10. Sprinkle pomegranate arils, toasted pumpkin seeds, and crumbled feta cheese (if using) over the bowls.
11. Finish the bowls with a drizzle of balsamic glaze.

Nutritional Information (Per Serving):

- **Carbs:** 45g

- **Fats:** 15g

- **Fiber:** 10g

- **Protein:** 12g

Thai Basil Coconut Millet Bowl with Crispy Tofu

Prep Time: 30 minutes
Cook Time: 30 minutes
Servings: 4

Ingredients:

For the Millet Bowl:

- 1 cup millet

- 2 cups coconut milk

- 1 cup water

- 1 red bell pepper (sliced)

- 1 zucchini (sliced)

- 1 carrot (julienned)

- 1 cup snap peas (sliced)

- 1 cup firm tofu (pressed and cubed)

- 2 tablespoons vegetable oil

- Sesame seeds for garnish

For the Thai Basil Sauce:

- ¼ cup soy sauce

- 2 tablespoons hoisin sauce

- 1 tablespoon rice vinegar

- 1 tablespoon maple syrup

- 1 tablespoon fresh ginger (minced)

- 2 cloves garlic (minced)

- ½ cup fresh Thai basil leaves

Directions:

Millet Bowl:

1. In a saucepan, add in the millet, coconut milk, and water.
2. Bring to a boil, then reduce heat, cover, and simmer for 20-25 minutes or until millet is cooked and liquid is absorbed.
3. In a large pan or wok, heat vegetable oil over medium-high heat.
4. Sauté sliced red bell pepper, sliced zucchini, julienned carrot, and sliced snap peas until tender-crisp.
5. In the same pan, add cubed tofu and cook until golden brown on all sides.
6. In a bowl, whisk together soy sauce, hoisin sauce, rice vinegar, maple syrup, minced ginger, minced garlic, and Thai basil leaves.
7. Pour the Thai Basil Sauce over the cooked vegetables and tofu in the pan.
8. Allow the mixture to simmer for 5 minutes, allowing the flavors to meld.
9. Divide the cooked millet among serving bowls.
10. Spoon the Thai basil-coated vegetables and crispy tofu over the millet.
11. Garnish with sesame seeds.

Nutritional Information (Per Serving):

- **Carbs:** 60g

- **Fats:** 20g

- **Fiber:** 10g

- **Protein:** 15g

Chapter 4: Flexi-Tacos

BBQ Jackfruit Tacos with Slaw

Prep Time: 15 minutes
Cook Time: 25 minutes
Servings: 4

Ingredients:

For BBQ Jackfruit:

- 2 cans (20 ounces each) young green jackfruit in water, drained and rinsed
- 1 cup barbecue sauce
- 1 tablespoon olive oil
- 1 teaspoon garlic powder
- 1 teaspoon onion powder
- ½ teaspoon smoked paprika
- Salt and pepper to taste

For Slaw:

- 2 cups shredded cabbage
- 1 cup shredded carrots
- ½ cup chopped fresh cilantro
- 2 tablespoons mayonnaise (vegan or traditional)
- 1 tablespoon apple cider vinegar
- Salt and pepper to taste

For Tacos:

- 8 small corn tortillas

Directions:

1. Heat olive oil in a large skillet over medium heat.
2. Add drained jackfruit and sauté for 2-3 minutes.
3. Add garlic powder, onion powder, smoked paprika, salt, and pepper. Stir to combine.
4. Pour in barbecue sauce and simmer for 15-20 minutes, stirring occasionally, until jackfruit is tender and well-coated in the sauce.

5. In a large bowl, add in the shredded cabbage, shredded carrots, and chopped cilantro.
6. In a small bowl, whisk together mayonnaise and apple cider vinegar, and stir to combine.
7. Pour the dressing over the cabbage mixture and toss until well coated. Season with salt and pepper to taste.
8. Warm corn tortillas in a dry skillet or microwave according to package instructions.
9. Assemble the tacos by spooning the BBQ jackfruit onto each tortilla and topping with slaw, and serve right away.

Nutritional Information (Per Serving):

- **Carbs:** 45g

- **Fats:** 10g

- **Fiber:** 8g

- **Protein:** 5g

Mushroom and Walnut Taco Filling

Prep Time: 15 minutes
Cook Time: 20 minutes
Servings: 4

Ingredients:

- 1 cup walnuts, chopped

- 1 tablespoon olive oil

- 1 onion, finely chopped

- 2 cloves garlic, minced

- 8 ounces cremini mushrooms, finely chopped

- 1 teaspoon cumin

- 1 teaspoon chili powder

- ½ teaspoon smoked paprika

- Salt and pepper to taste

- ¼ cup tomato paste

- ½ cup vegetable broth

- 2 tablespoons soy sauce

- 1 tablespoon lime juice

- 8 small corn tortillas

Directions:

1. In a large skillet, toast the chopped walnuts over medium heat until fragrant, about 3-4 minutes. Remove from the skillet and set aside.
2. In the same skillet, heat olive oil over medium heat. Add chopped onions and sauté until translucent.
3. Add minced garlic to the onions and sauté for an additional 1-2 minutes.
4. Add finely chopped cremini mushrooms to the skillet. Cook until mushrooms release their moisture and become golden brown.
5. Stir in cumin, chili powder, smoked paprika, salt, and pepper. Mix properly to coat the mushrooms.
6. Add tomato paste to the mushroom mixture and cook for 2-3 minutes.
7. Pour in vegetable broth, soy sauce, and lime juice. Stir to combine.
8. Add the toasted walnuts back to the skillet and cook for an additional 5-7 minutes until the mixture thickens and flavors meld.
9. Warm corn tortillas in a dry skillet or microwave according to package instructions.
10. Assemble the tacos by spooning the mushroom and walnut filling onto each tortilla.
11. Garnish with your favorite toppings and serve immediately.

Nutritional Information (Per Serving):

- **Carbs:** 30g

- **Fats:** 15g

- **Fiber:** 6g

- **Protein:** 8g

Tofu and Black Bean Tacos with Avocado Lime Crema

Prep Time: 20 minutes
Cook Time: 15 minutes
Servings: 4

Ingredients:

For Tofu and Black Bean Filling:

- 1 tablespoon olive oil

- 1 onion, finely diced

- 2 cloves garlic, minced

- 1 block (14 ounces) extra-firm tofu, pressed and crumbled

- 1 can (15 ounces) black beans, drained and rinsed

- 1 teaspoon ground cumin

- 1 teaspoon chili powder

- ½ teaspoon smoked paprika

- Salt and pepper to taste

- ¼ cup chopped fresh cilantro

For Avocado Lime Crema:

- 1 ripe avocado

- ¼ cup plain Greek yogurt (or non-dairy alternative)

- Juice of 1 lime

- Salt to taste

For Tacos:

- 8 small corn tortillas

- Additional toppings: shredded lettuce, diced tomatoes, salsa

Directions:

1. Heat olive oil in a large skillet over medium heat. Add diced onions and sauté until translucent.
2. Add minced garlic to the onions and sauté for an additional 1-2 minutes.
3. Crumble the pressed tofu into the skillet. Cook until tofu starts to brown.
4. Stir in black beans, cumin, chili powder, smoked paprika, salt, and pepper. Mix properly to combine.
5. Cook for an additional 5-7 minutes, allowing flavors to meld. Add chopped cilantro and mix.
6. In a blender or food processor, add in the avocado, Greek yogurt, lime juice, and salt. Blend until smooth and creamy.
7. Warm corn tortillas in a dry skillet or microwave according to package instructions.
8. Assemble the tacos by spooning the tofu and black bean filling onto each tortilla.
9. Top with shredded lettuce, diced tomatoes, salsa, and a drizzle of avocado lime crema, and serve right away.

Nutritional Information (Per Serving):

- **Carbs:** 35g

- **Fats:** 14g

- **Fiber:** 9g

- **Protein:** 15g

Greek-inspired Chickpea Gyro Tacos

Prep Time: 15 minutes
Cook Time: 15 minutes
Servings: 4

Ingredients:

For Chickpea Gyro Filling:

- 2 cans (15 ounces each) chickpeas, drained and rinsed

- 2 tablespoons olive oil

- 1 teaspoon dried oregano

- 1 teaspoon ground cumin

- 1 teaspoon smoked paprika

- Salt and pepper to taste

- 1 cup cherry tomatoes, halved

- 1 cucumber, diced

- ½ red onion, finely sliced

- ½ cup crumbled feta cheese (optional)

For Tzatziki Sauce:

- 1 cup Greek yogurt (or non-dairy alternative)

- 1 cucumber, grated and drained

- 2 cloves garlic, minced

- 1 tablespoon fresh dill, chopped

- Juice of 1 lemon

- Salt and pepper to taste

For Tacos:

- 8 small whole wheat or corn tortillas

Directions:

1. In a large skillet, heat olive oil over medium heat. Add chickpeas, dried oregano, ground cumin, smoked paprika, salt, and pepper. Sauté for 5-7 minutes until chickpeas are heated through and coated in the spices.
2. In a large bowl, add in the cherry tomatoes, diced cucumber, and finely sliced red onion.
3. Add the sautéed chickpeas to the bowl and toss to combine. If using, sprinkle crumbled feta cheese over the mixture.
4. In a medium bowl, add in the Greek yogurt, grated and drained cucumber, minced garlic, chopped fresh dill, lemon juice, salt, and pepper. Mix properly.
5. Warm whole wheat or corn tortillas in a dry skillet or microwave according to package instructions.
6. Assemble the tacos by spooning the chickpea gyro filling onto each tortilla.
7. Drizzle with tzatziki sauce, and serve right away.

Nutritional Information (Per Serving):

- **Carbs:** 45g

- **Fats:** 15g

- **Fiber:** 10g

- **Protein:** 15g

Cauliflower and Lentil Lettuce Wrap Tacos

Prep Time: 20 minutes
Cook Time: 25 minutes
Servings: 4

Ingredients:

For Cauliflower and Lentil Filling:

- 1 head cauliflower, finely chopped

- 1 cup dry green lentils, rinsed and drained

- 2 tablespoons olive oil

- 1 onion, finely diced

- 3 cloves garlic, minced

- 1 teaspoon ground cumin

- 1 teaspoon chili powder

- ½ teaspoon smoked paprika

- Salt and pepper to taste

- 1 cup cherry tomatoes, diced
- ½ cup fresh cilantro, chopped

For Avocado Lime Crema:

- 2 ripe avocados
- ¼ cup plain Greek yogurt (or non-dairy alternative)
- Juice of 2 limes
- Salt to taste

For Lettuce Wraps:

- 1 head iceberg lettuce, leaves separated

Directions:

Cauliflower and Lentil Filling:

1. In a food processor, pulse the cauliflower until it resembles rice-sized pieces.
2. In a large skillet, heat olive oil over medium heat. Add diced onions and sauté until translucent.
3. Add minced garlic to the onions and sauté for an additional 1-2 minutes.
4. Stir in finely chopped cauliflower and rinsed lentils. Add ground cumin, chili powder, smoked paprika, salt, and pepper. Cook for 15-20 minutes until cauliflower is tender and lentils are cooked through.
5. Add diced cherry tomatoes and chopped fresh cilantro. Mix properly.

Avocado Lime Crema:

1. In a blender or food processor, add in the ripe avocados, Greek yogurt, lime juice, and salt. Blend until smooth and creamy.

Lettuce Wraps:

1. Spoon the cauliflower and lentil filling onto individual iceberg lettuce leaves.
2. Drizzle with avocado lime crema and serve right away.

Nutritional Information (Per Serving):

- **Carbs:** 40g
- **Fats:** 15g
- **Fiber:** 15g
- **Protein:** 10g

Sweet Potato and Black Bean Tacos with Chipotle Crema

Prep Time: 20 minutes
Cook Time: 25 minutes
Servings: 4

Ingredients:

For Sweet Potato and Black Bean Filling:

- 2 large sweet potatoes, peeled and diced
- 2 tablespoons olive oil
- 1 teaspoon ground cumin
- 1 teaspoon chili powder
- ½ teaspoon smoked paprika
- Salt and pepper to taste
- 1 can (15 ounces) black beans, drained and rinsed
- 1 cup corn kernels (fresh, frozen, or canned)
- ¼ cup chopped fresh cilantro

For Chipotle Crema:

- ½ cup sour cream (or non-dairy alternative)
- 1 chipotle pepper in adobo sauce, minced
- 1 tablespoon adobo sauce (from the can of chipotle peppers)
- Juice of 1 lime
- Salt to taste

For Tacos:

- 8 small corn tortillas

Directions:

Sweet Potato and Black Bean Filling:

1. Preheat the oven to 400°F (200°C).

2. In a large bowl, toss diced sweet potatoes with olive oil, ground cumin, chili powder, smoked paprika, salt, and pepper.

3. Spread the seasoned sweet potatoes on a baking sheet in a single layer. Roast in the preheated oven for 20-25 minutes or until tender and slightly caramelized.

4. In a large skillet, add in the roasted sweet potatoes, drained black beans, corn kernels, and chopped cilantro. Heat through.

Chipotle Crema:

1. In a small bowl, mix together sour cream, minced chipotle pepper, adobo sauce, lime juice, and salt. Adjust seasoning to taste.

Tacos:

1. Warm corn tortillas in a dry skillet or microwave according to package instructions.

2. Assemble the tacos by spooning the sweet potato and black bean filling onto each tortilla.

3. Drizzle with chipotle crema and serve right away.

Nutritional Information (Per Serving):

- **Carbs:** 45g

- **Fats:** 15g

- **Fiber:** 10g

- **Protein:** 8g

Teriyaki Portobello Mushroom Tacos

Prep Time: 15 minutes
Cook Time: 20 minutes
Servings: 4

Ingredients:

For Teriyaki Portobello Mushrooms:

- 4 large Portobello mushrooms, cleaned and sliced

- ½ cup low-sodium soy sauce (or tamari for gluten-free)

- 2 tablespoons rice vinegar

- 2 tablespoons maple syrup

- 2 cloves garlic, minced

- 1 teaspoon fresh ginger, grated

- 1 tablespoon cornstarch

- 2 tablespoons water

- 2 tablespoons sesame oil

- Sesame seeds for garnish

For Slaw:

- 2 cups shredded cabbage

- 1 cup shredded carrots

- ½ cup chopped green onions

- 1 tablespoon rice vinegar

- 1 tablespoon sesame oil

- Salt and pepper to taste

For Tacos:

- 8 small flour or corn tortillas

Directions:

Teriyaki Portobello Mushrooms:

1. In a bowl, whisk together soy sauce, rice vinegar, maple syrup, minced garlic, and grated ginger.

2. In a small bowl, make a slurry by combining cornstarch and water.

3. Heat sesame oil in a large skillet over medium heat. Add sliced Portobello mushrooms and sauté until they release their moisture.

4. Pour the teriyaki sauce over the mushrooms and stir to coat. Cook for 5-7 minutes until the mushrooms are tender.

5. Add the cornstarch slurry to the skillet and cook for an additional 2-3 minutes, allowing the sauce to thicken.

6. Garnish with sesame seeds.

Slaw:

1. In a large bowl, add in the shredded cabbage, shredded carrots, chopped green onions, rice vinegar, sesame oil, salt, and pepper. Toss until well coated.

Tacos:

1. Warm flour or corn tortillas in a dry skillet or microwave according to package instructions.

2. Assemble the tacos by spooning the teriyaki Portobello mushrooms onto each tortilla.

3. Top with the slaw and serve right away.

Nutritional Information (Per Serving):

- **Carbs:** 45g

- **Fats:** 15g

- **Fiber:** 8g

- **Protein:** 10g

Pineapple and Quinoa Stuffed Pepper Tacos

Prep Time: 20 minutes
Cook Time: 35 minutes
Servings: 4

Ingredients:

For Pineapple and Quinoa Filling:

- 1 cup quinoa, rinsed

- 2 cups vegetable broth

- 4 large bell peppers, halved and seeds removed

- 1 tablespoon olive oil

- 1 onion, finely diced

- 2 cloves garlic, minced

- 1 cup black beans, cooked and drained

- 1 cup corn kernels (fresh, frozen, or canned)

- 1 cup diced pineapple

- 1 teaspoon ground cumin

- 1 teaspoon chili powder

- Salt and pepper to taste

- ¼ cup fresh cilantro, chopped

- 1 cup shredded cheese (cheddar, Monterey Jack, or a blend)

For Tacos:

- 8 small flour or corn tortillas
- Avocado slices for garnish
- Lime wedges for serving

Directions:

Pineapple and Quinoa Filling:

1. In a medium saucepan, add in the quinoa and vegetable broth. Bring to a boil, then reduce heat to low, cover, and simmer for 15-20 minutes or until quinoa is cooked and liquid is absorbed.

2. Preheat the oven to 375°F (190°C).

3. In a large skillet, heat olive oil over medium heat. Add finely diced onion and sauté until translucent.

4. Add minced garlic to the skillet and sauté for an additional 1-2 minutes.

5. Stir in black beans, corn kernels, diced pineapple, ground cumin, chili powder, salt, and pepper. Cook for 5-7 minutes until heated through.

6. Add cooked quinoa to the skillet and mix properly. Stir in chopped fresh cilantro.

Tacos:

1. Stuff each halved bell pepper with the pineapple and quinoa filling.

2. Place the stuffed peppers in a baking dish. Top each pepper with shredded cheese.

3. Bake in the preheated oven for 15-20 minutes or until the cheese is melted and bubbly.

4. Warm flour or corn tortillas in a dry skillet or microwave according to package instructions.

5. Assemble the tacos by placing a stuffed pepper into each tortilla.

6. Garnish with avocado slices and serve with lime wedges.

Nutritional Information (Per Serving):

- **Carbs:** 55g
- **Fats:** 15g
- **Fiber:** 12g
- **Protein:** 18g

Buffalo Cauliflower and Avocado Tacos

Prep Time: 20 minutes
Cook Time: 25 minutes
Servings: 4

Ingredients:

For Buffalo Cauliflower:

- 1 head cauliflower, cut into florets
- ½ cup all-purpose flour
- ½ cup milk (dairy or non-dairy)
- 1 teaspoon garlic powder
- 1 teaspoon onion powder
- ½ teaspoon smoked paprika
- Salt and pepper to taste
- ½ cup buffalo sauce
- 2 tablespoons unsalted butter (or vegan butter)

For Tacos:

- 8 small flour or corn tortillas
- 2 avocados, sliced
- Shredded lettuce for garnish
- Ranch dressing (dairy or non-dairy) for drizzling
- Fresh cilantro for topping

Directions:

Buffalo Cauliflower:

1. Preheat the oven to 450°F (230°C) and line a baking sheet with parchment paper.

2. In a bowl, whisk together flour, milk, garlic powder, onion powder, smoked paprika, salt, and pepper to create the batter.

3. Dip each cauliflower floret into the batter, ensuring it's well-coated, and place it on the prepared baking sheet.

4. Bake for 20 minutes or until the cauliflower is golden brown and crispy.

5. While the cauliflower is baking, in a small saucepan, heat buffalo sauce and butter over low heat until the butter is melted. Stir to combine.

6. Once the cauliflower is done baking, transfer it to a bowl and pour the buffalo sauce mixture over it. Toss until the cauliflower is evenly coated.

Tacos:

1. Warm flour or corn tortillas in a dry skillet or microwave according to package instructions.

2. Assemble the tacos by placing buffalo cauliflower in each tortilla.

3. Top with sliced avocados, shredded lettuce, and drizzle with ranch dressing.

4. Garnish with fresh cilantro and serve right away.

Nutritional Information (Per Serving):

- **Carbs:** 45g

- **Fats:** 20g

- **Fiber:** 10g

- **Protein:** 8g

Jamaican Jerk Cauliflower Tacos with Pineapple Salsa

Prep Time: 20 minutes
Cook Time: 25 minutes
Servings: 4

Ingredients:

For Jamaican Jerk Cauliflower:

- 1 head cauliflower, cut into florets

- 3 tablespoons olive oil

- 2 tablespoons Jamaican jerk seasoning

- 1 tablespoon soy sauce (or tamari for gluten-free)

- 1 tablespoon maple syrup

- 1 teaspoon garlic powder

- 1 teaspoon onion powder

- ½ teaspoon dried thyme

- Salt and pepper to taste

For Pineapple Salsa:

- 1 cup diced pineapple

- ½ red onion, finely diced

- 1 jalapeño, seeds removed and finely chopped

- ¼ cup chopped fresh cilantro

- Juice of 1 lime

- Salt to taste

For Tacos:

- 8 small flour or corn tortillas

- Shredded cabbage for garnish

- Lime wedges for serving

Directions:

Jamaican Jerk Cauliflower:

1. Preheat the oven to 425°F (220°C) and line a baking sheet with parchment paper.

2. In a bowl, add in the olive oil, Jamaican jerk seasoning, soy sauce, maple syrup, garlic powder, onion powder, dried thyme, salt, and pepper.

3. Toss cauliflower florets in the jerk seasoning mixture until well coated.

4. Spread the cauliflower on the prepared baking sheet and roast for 20-25 minutes or until golden brown and tender.

Pineapple Salsa:

1. In a bowl, add in the diced pineapple, finely diced red onion, chopped jalapeño, chopped fresh cilantro, lime juice, and salt. Mix properly.

Tacos:

1. Warm flour or corn tortillas in a dry skillet or microwave according to package instructions.

2. Assemble the tacos by placing Jamaican jerk cauliflower in each tortilla.

3. Top with shredded cabbage and a generous spoonful of pineapple salsa.

4. Serve with lime wedges on the side.

Nutritional Information (Per Serving):

- **Carbs:** 40g

- **Fats:** 15g

- **Fiber:** 8g

- **Protein:** 6g

Harissa Spiced Lentil and Cucumber Yogurt Tacos

Prep Time: 20 minutes
Cook Time: 25 minutes
Servings: 4

Ingredients:

For Harissa Spiced Lentils:

- 1 cup dry green lentils, rinsed and drained

- 2 cups vegetable broth

- 2 tablespoons olive oil

- 1 onion, finely diced

- 2 cloves garlic, minced

- 2 tablespoons harissa paste

- 1 teaspoon ground cumin

- 1 teaspoon ground coriander

- ½ teaspoon smoked paprika

- Salt and pepper to taste

For Cucumber Yogurt Sauce:

- 1 cucumber, finely diced

- 1 cup Greek yogurt (or non-dairy alternative)

- 1 tablespoon fresh mint, chopped

- 1 tablespoon fresh cilantro, chopped

- Juice of 1 lemon

- Salt and pepper to taste

For Tacos:

- 8 small flour or corn tortillas
- Sliced radishes for garnish
- Fresh mint and cilantro for topping

Directions:

Harissa Spiced Lentils:

1. In a saucepan, add in the dry green lentils and vegetable broth. Bring to a boil, then reduce heat to low, cover, and simmer for 15-20 minutes or until lentils are tender.

2. In a skillet, heat olive oil over medium heat. Add finely diced onion and sauté until translucent.

3. Add minced garlic to the skillet and sauté for an additional 1-2 minutes.

4. Stir in harissa paste, ground cumin, ground coriander, smoked paprika, salt, and pepper. Cook for 2-3 minutes.

5. Add cooked lentils to the skillet and mix properly. Cook for an additional 5-7 minutes, allowing the flavors to meld.

Cucumber Yogurt Sauce:

1. In a bowl, add in the finely diced cucumber, Greek yogurt, chopped fresh mint, chopped fresh cilantro, lemon juice, salt, and pepper. Mix properly.

Tacos:

1. Warm flour or corn tortillas in a dry skillet or microwave according to package instructions.

2. Assemble the tacos by spooning harissa spiced lentils onto each tortilla.

3. Top with cucumber yogurt sauce.

4. Garnish with sliced radishes, fresh mint, and cilantro, and serve right away.

Nutritional Information (Per Serving):

- **Carbs:** 45g
- **Fats:** 12g
- **Fiber:** 12g
- **Protein:** 14g

Miso Glazed Eggplant and Avocado Tacos

Prep Time: 20 minutes
Cook Time: 25 minutes
Servings: 4

Ingredients:

For Miso Glazed Eggplant:

- 2 large eggplants, sliced
- 2 tablespoons olive oil
- 2 tablespoons white miso paste
- 1 tablespoon soy sauce (or tamari for gluten-free)
- 1 tablespoon maple syrup
- 1 teaspoon sesame oil
- 2 cloves garlic, minced
- 1 teaspoon grated ginger
- Sesame seeds for garnish

For Tacos:

- 8 small flour or corn tortillas
- 2 avocados, sliced
- Shredded red cabbage for garnish
- Green onions, sliced, for topping

Directions:

Miso Glazed Eggplant:

1. Preheat the oven to 400°F (200°C) and line a baking sheet with parchment paper.

2. In a bowl, whisk together olive oil, white miso paste, soy sauce, maple syrup, sesame oil, minced garlic, and grated ginger.

3. Brush the miso glaze onto each side of the eggplant slices and place them on the prepared baking sheet.

4. Bake for 20-25 minutes or until the eggplant is tender and golden brown.

5. Garnish with sesame seeds.

Tacos:

1. Warm flour or corn tortillas in a dry skillet or microwave according to package instructions.

2. Assemble the tacos by placing miso glazed eggplant slices onto each tortilla.

3. Top with sliced avocados, shredded red cabbage, and sliced green onions, and serve right away.

Nutritional Information (Per Serving):

- **Carbs:** 50g

- **Fats:** 20g

- **Fiber:** 15g

- **Protein:** 8g

Caprese Style Pesto Quinoa Tacos with Balsamic Reduction

Prep Time: 20 minutes
Cook Time: 20 minutes
Servings: 4

Ingredients:

For Pesto Quinoa:

- 1 cup quinoa, rinsed and drained

- 2 cups vegetable broth

- 3 tablespoons pesto sauce

- Salt and pepper to taste

For Tacos:

- 8 small flour or corn tortillas

- 2 cups cherry tomatoes, halved

- 1 cup fresh mozzarella balls, halved

- ½ cup fresh basil leaves

- Balsamic reduction for drizzling

- Olive oil for drizzling

- Salt and pepper to taste

Directions:

Pesto Quinoa:

1. In a saucepan, add in the quinoa and vegetable broth. Bring to a boil, then reduce heat to low, cover, and simmer for 15-20 minutes or until quinoa is cooked and liquid is absorbed.

2. Fluff the quinoa with a fork and stir in pesto sauce. Season with salt and pepper to taste.

Tacos:

1. Warm flour or corn tortillas in a dry skillet or microwave according to package instructions.

2. Assemble the tacos by spooning pesto quinoa onto each tortilla.

3. Top with halved cherry tomatoes, halved fresh mozzarella balls, and fresh basil leaves.

4. Drizzle with balsamic reduction and olive oil.

5. Season with salt and pepper to taste, and serve right away.

Nutritional Information (Per Serving):

- **Carbs:** 55g
- **Fats:** 20g
- **Fiber:** 8g
- **Protein:** 15g

Chapter 5: Veggie-Packed Stir-Fries

Sesame Ginger Tofu and Broccoli Stir-Fry

Prep Time: 15 minutes
Cook Time: 20 minutes
Number of Servings: 4

Ingredients:

- 1 pound firm tofu, cubed

- 4 cups broccoli florets

- 1 red bell pepper, thinly sliced

- 1 yellow bell pepper, thinly sliced

- 1 cup snow peas, ends trimmed

- ¼ cup soy sauce

- 2 tablespoons sesame oil

- 3 tablespoons hoisin sauce

- 2 tablespoons rice vinegar

- 1 tablespoon ginger, minced

- 3 cloves garlic, minced

- 2 tablespoons sesame seeds, toasted

- 2 green onions, sliced

- 2 cups cooked brown rice or quinoa

Directions:

1. **Preparation:** Press the tofu to remove excess water, then cube it.

2. **Stir-Fry:** Heat a large skillet or wok over medium-high heat. Add 1 tablespoon of sesame oil. Add the tofu cubes and cook until golden brown on all sides. Remove tofu from the skillet and set aside.

3. **Vegetable Medley:** In the same skillet, add another tablespoon of sesame oil. Add the broccoli, red bell pepper, yellow bell pepper, and snow peas. Stir-fry until the vegetables are crisp-tender.

4. **Sauce:** In a small bowl, whisk together soy sauce, hoisin sauce, rice vinegar, minced ginger, and minced garlic. Pour the sauce over the vegetable mixture.

5. **Combine and Toast:** Add the cooked tofu back to the skillet. Toss everything together until well-coated in the sauce. Allow it to cook for an additional 2-3 minutes to heat through.

6. **Serve:** Sprinkle with toasted sesame seeds and sliced green onions. Serve the stir-fry over cooked brown rice or quinoa.

Nutritional Information (Per Serving):

- Carbs: 45g

- Fats: 14g

- Fiber: 8g

- Protein: 18g

Coconut Curry Tempeh and Vegetable Stir-Fry

Prep Time: 20 minutes
Cook Time: 25 minutes
Number of Servings: 4

Ingredients:

- 1 package (8 ounces) tempeh, cut into cubes

- 4 cups mixed vegetables (e.g., bell peppers, broccoli, carrots), sliced

- 1 can (14 ounces) coconut milk

- 3 tablespoons red curry paste

- 2 tablespoons soy sauce

- 1 tablespoon coconut oil

- 1 tablespoon maple syrup

- 1 tablespoon ginger, minced

- 3 cloves garlic, minced

- 1 lime, juiced

- Fresh cilantro, for garnish

- Cooked quinoa or rice, for serving

Directions:

1. **Tempeh Prep:** Steam the tempeh cubes for 10 minutes to reduce bitterness. Set aside.

2. **Stir-Fry Base:** In a large skillet or wok, heat coconut oil over medium heat. Add minced ginger and garlic, sautéing until fragrant.

3. **Tempeh Addition:** Add the steamed tempeh cubes to the skillet. Cook until golden brown on all sides.

4. **Vegetable Medley:** Add the sliced mixed vegetables to the skillet. Stir-fry until the vegetables are tender-crisp.

5. **Curry Sauce:** In a bowl, whisk together coconut milk, red curry paste, soy sauce, maple syrup, and lime juice. Pour the sauce over the tempeh and vegetables.

6. **Combine the Ingredients and Simmer:** Stir everything together and let it simmer for 10-15 minutes, allowing the flavors to meld and the sauce to thicken.

7. **Serve:** Serve the stir-fry over cooked quinoa or rice. Garnish with fresh cilantro.

Nutritional Information (Per Serving):

- Carbs: 32g

- Fats: 20g

- Fiber: 7g

- Protein: 15g

Cashew and Vegetable Teriyaki Stir-Fry

Prep Time: 15 minutes
Cook Time: 20 minutes
Number of Servings: 4

Ingredients:

- 1 cup cashews

- 1 pound mixed vegetables (e.g., broccoli, bell peppers, carrots), sliced

- 1 block (14 ounces) firm tofu, cubed

- ½ cup low-sodium soy sauce

- 3 tablespoons teriyaki sauce

- 2 tablespoons rice vinegar

- 2 tablespoons maple syrup

- 1 tablespoon cornstarch

- 2 tablespoons vegetable oil

- 1 tablespoon ginger, minced

- 3 cloves garlic, minced

- 2 green onions, sliced

- Sesame seeds, for garnish

- Cooked brown rice, for serving

Directions:

1. **Cashew Toasting:** In a dry skillet over medium heat, toast the cashews until golden brown. Set aside.

2. **Vegetable and Tofu Prep:** In a large wok or skillet, heat vegetable oil over medium-high heat. Add the sliced mixed vegetables and cubed tofu. Stir-fry until the vegetables are tender-crisp and the tofu is golden brown.

3. **Teriyaki Sauce:** In a bowl, whisk together soy sauce, teriyaki sauce, rice vinegar, maple syrup, and cornstarch. Pour the sauce over the vegetable and tofu mixture.

4. **Combine the Ingredients and Simmer:** Stir everything together and let it simmer for 5-7 minutes, allowing the sauce to thicken and coat the ingredients.

5. **Flavor Infusion:** Add minced ginger and garlic to the wok. Stir-fry for an additional 2 minutes until fragrant.

6. **Serve:** Serve the stir-fry over cooked brown rice. Top with toasted cashews, sliced green onions, and a sprinkle of sesame seeds.

Nutritional Information (Per Serving):

- Carbs: 45g

- Fats: 18g

- Fiber: 8g

- Protein: 20g

Peanut Sauce Quinoa and Edamame Stir-Fry

Prep Time: 15 minutes
Cook Time: 20 minutes
Number of Servings: 4

Ingredients:

- 1 cup quinoa, rinsed
- 2 cups edamame, shelled
- 1 red bell pepper, thinly sliced
- 1 carrot, julienned
- 1 zucchini, sliced
- 1 cup shredded cabbage
- ½ cup peanuts, chopped
- 2 tablespoons vegetable oil
- 2 cloves garlic, minced
- 1 tablespoon ginger, minced
- ½ cup low-sodium soy sauce
- 3 tablespoons peanut butter
- 2 tablespoons rice vinegar
- 1 tablespoon maple syrup
- 1 teaspoon sesame oil
- 2 green onions, sliced
- Lime wedges, for serving

Directions:

1. **Quinoa:** Cook quinoa according to package instructions. Set aside.

2. **Edamame and Vegetable Prep:** In a large wok or skillet, heat vegetable oil over medium-high heat. Add minced garlic and ginger. Sauté until fragrant. Add sliced red bell pepper, julienned carrot, sliced zucchini, and shredded cabbage. Stir-fry until vegetables are tender-crisp.

3. **Peanut Sauce:** In a bowl, whisk together soy sauce, peanut butter, rice vinegar, maple syrup, and sesame oil. Pour the peanut sauce over the vegetable mixture.

4. **Quinoa and Edamame Addition:** Add the cooked quinoa and shelled edamame to the wok. Stir everything together until well-coated in the peanut sauce.

5. **Serve:** Garnish with chopped peanuts and sliced green onions. Serve with lime wedges on the side for an extra burst of flavor.

Nutritional Information (Per Serving):

- Carbs: 50g

- Fats: 20g

- Fiber: 12g

- Protein: 18g

Spicy Sriracha Eggplant and Tofu Stir-Fry

Prep Time: 20 minutes
Cook Time: 25 minutes
Number of Servings: 4

Ingredients:

- 1 large eggplant, diced

- 1 block (14 ounces) firm tofu, pressed and cubed

- 1 red bell pepper, sliced

- 1 yellow bell pepper, sliced

- ¼ cup soy sauce

- 2 tablespoons sriracha sauce

- 1 tablespoon maple syrup

- 1 tablespoon rice vinegar

- 1 tablespoon cornstarch

- 2 tablespoons vegetable oil

- 1 tablespoon ginger, minced

- 3 cloves garlic, minced

- Green onions, sliced, for garnish

- Sesame seeds, for garnish

- Cooked brown rice, for serving

Directions:

1. **Eggplant and Tofu Prep:** Press the tofu to remove excess water, then cube it. Dice the eggplant into bite-sized pieces.

2. **Stir-Fry Base:** In a large wok or skillet, heat vegetable oil over medium-high heat. Add minced ginger and garlic. Sauté until fragrant.

3. **Tofu and Eggplant Addition:** Add the cubed tofu and diced eggplant to the skillet. Stir-fry until the tofu is golden brown and the eggplant is tender.

4. **Sauce:** In a bowl, whisk together soy sauce, sriracha sauce, maple syrup, rice vinegar, and cornstarch. Pour the sauce over the tofu and eggplant mixture.

5. **Bell Peppers:** Add sliced red and yellow bell peppers to the wok. Stir-fry until the vegetables are crisp-tender.

6. **Combine the Ingredients and Simmer:** Stir everything together and let it simmer for 5-7 minutes, allowing the sauce to thicken and coat the ingredients.

7. **Serve:** Serve the spicy stir-fry over cooked brown rice. Garnish with sliced green onions and sesame seeds.

Nutritional Information (Per Serving):

- Carbs: 38g

- Fats: 16g

- Fiber: 9g

- Protein: 16g

Orange Glazed Cauliflower and Snap Pea Stir-Fry

Prep Time: 15 minutes
Cook Time: 20 minutes
Number of Servings: 4

Ingredients:

- 1 large cauliflower, cut into florets

- 2 cups snap peas, ends trimmed

- 1 red bell pepper, thinly sliced

- 1 yellow bell pepper, thinly sliced

- ½ cup orange juice

- ¼ cup low-sodium soy sauce

- 2 tablespoons rice vinegar

- 2 tablespoons maple syrup

- 1 tablespoon cornstarch

- 2 tablespoons vegetable oil

- 1 tablespoon ginger, minced

- 3 cloves garlic, minced

- Sesame seeds, for garnish

- Green onions, sliced, for garnish

- Cooked quinoa or rice, for serving

Directions:

1. **Vegetable Prep:** Cut cauliflower into florets, trim snap peas, and thinly slice red and yellow bell peppers.

2. **Stir-Fry Base:** In a large wok or skillet, heat vegetable oil over medium-high heat. Add minced ginger and garlic. Sauté until fragrant.

3. **Cauliflower and Snap Peas Addition:** Add cauliflower florets and snap peas to the skillet. Stir-fry until the vegetables are tender-crisp.

4. **Sauce:** In a bowl, whisk together orange juice, soy sauce, rice vinegar, maple syrup, and cornstarch. Pour the sauce over the vegetables.

5. **Bell Peppers:** Add sliced red and yellow bell peppers to the wok. Stir-fry until the peppers are crisp-tender.

6. **Combine the Ingredients and Simmer:** Stir everything together and let it simmer for 5-7 minutes, allowing the sauce to thicken and coat the vegetables.

7. **Serve:** Serve the stir-fry over cooked quinoa or rice. Garnish with sesame seeds and sliced green onions.

Nutritional Information (Per Serving):

- Carbs: 45g

- Fats: 8g

- Fiber: 9g

- Protein: 10g

Thai Basil Tempeh and Bell Pepper Stir-Fry

Prep Time: 15 minutes
Cook Time: 20 minutes
Number of Servings: 4

Ingredients:

- 1 package (8 ounces) tempeh, cut into cubes
- 2 red bell peppers, thinly sliced
- 1 yellow bell pepper, thinly sliced
- 1 cup fresh basil leaves, torn
- ¼ cup soy sauce
- 2 tablespoons oyster sauce
- 1 tablespoon fish sauce
- 1 tablespoon maple syrup
- 2 tablespoons vegetable oil
- 1 tablespoon ginger, minced
- 3 cloves garlic, minced
- 1 red chili, thinly sliced (optional)
- Cooked jasmine rice, for serving

Directions:

1. **Tempeh Prep:** Cut tempeh into cubes.

2. **Stir-Fry Base:** In a large wok or skillet, heat vegetable oil over medium-high heat. Add minced ginger and garlic. Sauté until fragrant.

3. **Tempeh Addition:** Add tempeh cubes to the skillet. Stir-fry until the tempeh is golden brown on all sides.

4. **Bell Peppers:** Add thinly sliced red and yellow bell peppers to the wok. Stir-fry until the vegetables are tender-crisp.

5. **Sauce:** In a bowl, whisk together soy sauce, oyster sauce, fish sauce, and maple syrup. Pour the sauce over the tempeh and bell peppers.

6. **Basil and Chili Addition:** Add torn fresh basil leaves and sliced red chili (if using) to the wok. Stir-fry until the basil wilts.

7. **Combine and Serve:** Stir everything together, making sure the tempeh and vegetables are coated in the sauce. Serve the stir-fry over cooked jasmine rice.

Nutritional Information (Per Serving):

- Carbs: 32g

- Fats: 14g

- Fiber: 6g

- Protein: 18g

Pineapple Fried Rice with Tofu

Prep Time: 20 minutes
Cook Time: 25 minutes
Number of Servings: 4

Ingredients:

- 2 cups cooked jasmine rice, cooled

- 1 cup pineapple, diced

- 1 block (14 ounces) firm tofu, pressed and cubed

- 1 cup frozen peas, thawed

- 1 red bell pepper, diced

- 1 carrot, diced

- 2 green onions, sliced

- ¼ cup soy sauce

- 2 tablespoons sesame oil

- 1 tablespoon curry powder

- 1 teaspoon turmeric

- 2 tablespoons vegetable oil

- 3 cloves garlic, minced

- 1 tablespoon ginger, minced

- Cashews or peanuts, for garnish (optional)

- Fresh cilantro, for garnish (optional)

- Lime wedges, for serving

Directions:

1. **Tofu Prep:** Press the tofu to remove excess water, then cut it into cubes.

2. **Stir-Fry Base:** In a large wok or skillet, heat vegetable oil over medium-high heat. Add minced ginger and garlic. Sauté until fragrant.

3. **Tofu and Vegetables:** Add cubed tofu, diced red bell pepper, and diced carrot to the skillet. Stir-fry until the tofu is golden brown and the vegetables are tender.

4. **Rice and Pineapple Addition:** Add cooked and cooled jasmine rice, diced pineapple, and thawed peas to the wok. Stir everything together.

5. **Sauce:** In a small bowl, mix soy sauce, sesame oil, curry powder, and turmeric. Pour the sauce over the rice and tofu mixture.

6. **Green Onions:** Add sliced green onions to the wok. Stir-fry for an additional 2-3 minutes until everything is well-coated.

7. **Garnish and Serve:** Garnish with cashews or peanuts and fresh cilantro if desired. Serve the pineapple fried rice with lime wedges on the side.

Nutritional Information (Per Serving):

- Carbs: 50g

- Fats: 18g

- Fiber: 7g

- Protein: 15g

Lemon Garlic Chickpea and Asparagus Stir-Fry

Prep Time: 15 minutes
Cook Time: 20 minutes
Number of Servings: 4

Ingredients:

- 2 cans (15 ounces each) chickpeas, drained and rinsed

- 1 bunch asparagus, trimmed and sliced

- 1 lemon, zested and juiced

- 3 tablespoons olive oil

- 4 cloves garlic, minced

- 1 teaspoon dried thyme

- Salt and pepper to taste

- Crushed red pepper flakes, for heat (optional)

- Fresh parsley, chopped, for garnish

- Cooked quinoa or couscous, for serving

Directions:

1. **Asparagus Prep:** Trim and slice the asparagus into bite-sized pieces.

2. **Chickpea and Asparagus Base:** In a large skillet or wok, heat olive oil over medium-high heat. Add minced garlic and sauté until fragrant. Add chickpeas and sliced asparagus. Stir-fry until the asparagus is tender-crisp.

3. **Lemon Zest and Juice:** Add lemon zest and juice to the skillet. Stir to combine, ensuring the chickpeas and asparagus are coated.

4. **Seasoning:** Sprinkle dried thyme over the mixture. Season with salt, pepper, and optional crushed red pepper flakes for heat.

5. **Combine and Heat Through:** Stir everything together and let it cook for an additional 2-3 minutes to allow the flavors to meld and the ingredients to heat through.

6. **Serve:** Serve the stir-fry over cooked quinoa or couscous. Garnish with fresh chopped parsley.

Nutritional Information (Per Serving):

- Carbs: 40g

- Fats: 12g

- Fiber: 12g

- Protein: 14g

Hoisin Glazed Portobello Mushroom Stir-Fry

Prep Time: 15 minutes
Cook Time: 20 minutes
Number of Servings: 4

Ingredients:

- 4 large Portobello mushrooms, sliced

- 1 red bell pepper, thinly sliced

- 1 yellow bell pepper, thinly sliced

- 1 cup snap peas, ends trimmed

- ½ cup sliced water chestnuts, drained

- ¼ cup hoisin sauce

- 2 tablespoons soy sauce

- 1 tablespoon rice vinegar

- 1 tablespoon sesame oil

- 2 tablespoons vegetable oil

- 1 tablespoon ginger, minced

- 3 cloves garlic, minced

- Green onions, sliced, for garnish

- Sesame seeds, for garnish

- Cooked brown rice or noodles, for serving

Directions:

1. **Mushroom Prep:** Clean and slice the Portobello mushrooms.

2. **Stir-Fry Base:** In a large wok or skillet, heat vegetable oil over medium-high heat. Add minced ginger and garlic. Sauté until fragrant.

3. **Portobello and Vegetables:** Add sliced Portobello mushrooms, red bell pepper, yellow bell pepper, snap peas, and water chestnuts to the skillet. Stir-fry until the vegetables are tender-crisp.

4. **Hoisin Glaze:** In a bowl, whisk together hoisin sauce, soy sauce, rice vinegar, and sesame oil. Pour the hoisin glaze over the mushroom and vegetable mixture.

5. **Combine and Heat Through:** Stir everything together, ensuring the mushrooms and vegetables are well-coated in the hoisin glaze. Cook for an additional 2-3 minutes to heat through.

6. **Serve:** Serve the stir-fry over cooked brown rice or noodles. Garnish with sliced green onions and sesame seeds.

Nutritional Information (Per Serving):

- Carbs: 30g

- Fats: 8g

- Fiber: 7g

- Protein: 6g

Mango and Cashew Coconut Rice Stir-Fry

Prep Time: 20 minutes
Cook Time: 25 minutes
Number of Servings: 4

Ingredients:

- 2 cups jasmine rice, cooked and cooled

- 1 ripe mango, peeled and diced

- 1 cup snow peas, ends trimmed

- 1 red bell pepper, thinly sliced

- 1 carrot, julienned

- ½ cup unsweetened coconut flakes

- ½ cup cashews

- ¼ cup soy sauce

- 2 tablespoons sesame oil

- 1 tablespoon maple syrup

- 1 tablespoon rice vinegar

- 2 tablespoons vegetable oil

- 3 cloves garlic, minced

- 1 tablespoon ginger, minced

- Fresh cilantro, chopped, for garnish

Directions:

1. **Rice Prep:** Cook jasmine rice according to package instructions. Allow it to cool.

2. **Stir-Fry Base:** In a large wok or skillet, heat vegetable oil over medium-high heat. Add minced garlic and ginger. Sauté until fragrant.

3. **Vegetable and Mango Addition:** Add snow peas, sliced red bell pepper, julienned carrot, and diced mango to the skillet. Stir-fry until the vegetables are tender-crisp.

4. **Coconut and Cashews:** Add unsweetened coconut flakes and cashews to the wok. Continue to stir-fry until the coconut is lightly toasted.

5. **Sauce:** In a bowl, whisk together soy sauce, sesame oil, maple syrup, and rice vinegar. Pour the sauce over the vegetable and mango mixture.

6. **Combine and Heat Through:** Add the cooled jasmine rice to the skillet. Stir everything together, ensuring the rice is well-coated in the sauce. Cook for an additional 2-3 minutes to heat through.

7. **Serve:** Garnish the stir-fry with chopped fresh cilantro.

Nutritional Information (Per Serving):

- Carbs: 60g

- Fats: 20g

- Fiber: 7g

- Protein: 10g

Turmeric Roasted Cauliflower and Chickpea Stir-Fry

Prep Time: 15 minutes
Cook Time: 30 minutes
Number of Servings: 4

Ingredients:

- 1 head cauliflower, cut into florets

- 1 can (15 ounces) chickpeas, drained and rinsed

- 1 red bell pepper, sliced

- 1 yellow bell pepper, sliced

- 1 onion, thinly sliced

- 2 tablespoons olive oil

- 1 teaspoon ground turmeric

- 1 teaspoon cumin

- 1 teaspoon paprika

- Salt and pepper to taste

- 2 tablespoons tahini

- 2 tablespoons lemon juice

- Fresh parsley, chopped, for garnish

- Cooked quinoa or rice, for serving

Directions:

1. **Cauliflower and Chickpea Prep:** Cut the cauliflower into florets and drain and rinse the chickpeas.

2. **Roasting:** Preheat the oven to 400°F (200°C). In a large baking sheet, add in the cauliflower florets, chickpeas, sliced red bell pepper, sliced yellow bell pepper, and thinly sliced onion. Drizzle with olive oil and sprinkle with ground turmeric, cumin, paprika, salt, and pepper. Toss everything to coat evenly. Roast in the oven for about 25-30 minutes or until the cauliflower is golden brown and tender.

3. **Tahini Sauce:** In a small bowl, mix tahini and lemon juice to create a sauce.

4. **Combine and Serve:** Once the roasted cauliflower and chickpeas are done, transfer them to a large skillet. Drizzle the tahini sauce over the mixture. Stir everything together and cook for an additional 2-3 minutes until heated through.

5. **Garnish and Serve:** Garnish the stir-fry with chopped fresh parsley. Serve over cooked quinoa or rice.

Nutritional Information (Per Serving):

- Carbs: 35g

- Fats: 12g

- Fiber: 10g

- Protein: 10g

Raspberry Teriyaki Tempeh and Snow Pea Stir-Fry

Prep Time: 20 minutes
Cook Time: 25 minutes
Number of Servings: 4

Ingredients:

- 1 package (8 ounces) tempeh, cut into cubes

- 2 cups snow peas, ends trimmed

- 1 red bell pepper, thinly sliced

- 1 yellow bell pepper, thinly sliced

- 1 cup fresh raspberries

- ¼ cup low-sodium soy sauce

- 2 tablespoons teriyaki sauce

- 2 tablespoons rice vinegar

- 2 tablespoons maple syrup

- 1 tablespoon cornstarch

- 2 tablespoons vegetable oil

- 1 tablespoon ginger, minced

- 3 cloves garlic, minced

- Cooked brown rice, for serving

- Sesame seeds, for garnish

- Green onions, sliced, for garnish

Directions:

1. **Tempeh Prep:** Cut tempeh into cubes.

2. **Stir-Fry Base:** In a large wok or skillet, heat vegetable oil over medium-high heat. Add minced ginger and garlic. Sauté until fragrant.

3. **Tempeh and Vegetables:** Add cubed tempeh, snow peas, sliced red bell pepper, and sliced yellow bell pepper to the skillet. Stir-fry until the tempeh is golden brown and the vegetables are tender-crisp.

4. **Raspberry Addition:** Add fresh raspberries to the wok. Gently stir to combine without breaking the raspberries.

5. **Sauce:** In a bowl, whisk together soy sauce, teriyaki sauce, rice vinegar, maple syrup, and cornstarch. Pour the sauce over the tempeh and vegetable mixture.

6. **Combine the Ingredients and Simmer:** Stir everything together and let it simmer for 5-7 minutes, allowing the sauce to thicken and coat the ingredients.

7. **Serve:** Serve the stir-fry over cooked brown rice. Garnish with sesame seeds and sliced green onions.

Nutritional Information (Per Serving):

- Carbs: 35g

- Fats: 15g

- Fiber: 8g

- Protein: 15g

Sesame Orange Glazed Broccoli and Quinoa Stir-Fry

Prep Time: 15 minutes
Cook Time: 20 minutes
Number of Servings: 4

Ingredients:

- 1 cup quinoa, rinsed
- 1 head broccoli, cut into florets
- 1 red bell pepper, thinly sliced
- 1 yellow bell pepper, thinly sliced
- ¼ cup sesame seeds
- 2 tablespoons vegetable oil
- ½ cup low-sodium soy sauce
- ¼ cup orange juice
- 2 tablespoons rice vinegar
- 2 tablespoons maple syrup
- 1 tablespoon cornstarch
- 2 teaspoons sesame oil
- 1 tablespoon ginger, minced
- 3 cloves garlic, minced
- Orange zest, for garnish
- Green onions, sliced, for garnish

Directions:

1. **Quinoa Prep:** Cook quinoa according to package instructions. Set aside.
2. **Stir-Fry Base:** In a large wok or skillet, heat vegetable oil over medium-high heat. Add minced ginger and garlic. Sauté until fragrant.
3. **Broccoli and Peppers:** Add broccoli florets, sliced red bell pepper, and sliced yellow bell pepper to the skillet. Stir-fry until the vegetables are tender-crisp.
4. **Sauce:** In a bowl, whisk together soy sauce, orange juice, rice vinegar, maple syrup, sesame oil, and cornstarch. Pour the sauce over the broccoli and pepper mixture.
5. **Sesame Seeds:** Add sesame seeds to the wok. Stir everything together.

6. **Combine the Ingredients and Simmer:** Let the stir-fry simmer for 5-7 minutes, allowing the sauce to thicken and coat the vegetables.

7. **Serve:** Serve the stir-fry over cooked quinoa. Garnish with orange zest and sliced green onions.

Nutritional Information (Per Serving):

- Carbs: 45g

- Fats: 15g

- Fiber: 8g

- Protein: 12g

Chapter 6: Protein-Packed Pastas

Lentil and Spinach Stuffed Shells

Prep Time: 25 minutes

Cook Time: 45 minutes

Servings: 6

Ingredients:

- 1 cup dried green lentils
- 1 pound jumbo pasta shells
- 2 tablespoons olive oil
- 1 onion, finely chopped
- 3 cloves garlic, minced
- 5 cups fresh spinach, chopped
- 1 teaspoon dried oregano
- 1 teaspoon dried basil
- ½ teaspoon salt
- ¼ teaspoon black pepper
- 1 can (28 ounces) crushed tomatoes
- 1 cup ricotta cheese
- 1 cup mozzarella cheese, shredded
- ½ cup Parmesan cheese, grated
- Fresh basil leaves for garnish (optional)

Directions:

1. Cook the lentils according to package instructions. Drain and set aside.

2. Cook the jumbo pasta shells al dente according to package instructions. Drain and set aside.

3. In a large skillet, heat olive oil over medium heat. Add chopped onion and sauté until translucent.

4. Add minced garlic to the skillet and sauté for an additional 1-2 minutes until fragrant.

5. Stir in chopped spinach and cook until wilted. Add oregano, basil, salt, and black pepper. Mix properly.

6. Pour crushed tomatoes into the skillet, stirring to combine. Allow the mixture to simmer for 10-15 minutes.

7. Preheat the oven to 350°F (175°C).

8. In a large mixing bowl, add in the cooked lentils, ricotta cheese, and ½ cup of mozzarella cheese. Mix properly.

9. Stuff each cooked pasta shell with the lentil and cheese mixture.

10. Spread a layer of the tomato and spinach sauce in a baking dish. Arrange the stuffed shells in the dish.

11. Top the shells with the remaining mozzarella and Parmesan cheeses.

12. Bake in the preheated oven for 25-30 minutes or until the cheese is melted and bubbly.

13. Garnish with fresh basil leaves, if desired, and serve hot.

Nutritional Information (Per Serving):

- Carbs: 54g

- Fats: 14g

- Fiber: 9g

- Protein: 21g

Chickpea and Artichoke Linguine

Prep Time: 15 minutes

Cook Time: 20 minutes

Servings: 4

Ingredients:

- 12 ounces linguine pasta

- 2 tablespoons olive oil

- 1 onion, finely diced

- 3 cloves garlic, minced

- 1 can (15 ounces) chickpeas, drained and rinsed

- 1 can (14 ounces) artichoke hearts, drained and quartered

- 1 teaspoon dried thyme

- ½ teaspoon red pepper flakes

- Salt and black pepper to taste

- 1 cup cherry tomatoes, halved

- ¼ cup fresh parsley, chopped

- ¼ cup grated Parmesan cheese (optional)

Directions:

1. Cook linguine pasta according to package instructions. Drain and set aside.

2. In a large skillet, heat olive oil over medium heat. Add finely diced onion and sauté until translucent.

3. Add minced garlic to the skillet and sauté for an additional 1-2 minutes until fragrant.

4. Stir in drained and rinsed chickpeas, quartered artichoke hearts, dried thyme, red pepper flakes, salt, and black pepper. Mix properly.

5. Cook the chickpea and artichoke mixture for 5-7 minutes, allowing the flavors to meld.

6. Add the halved cherry tomatoes to the skillet, cooking for an additional 2-3 minutes until the tomatoes are slightly softened.

7. Toss the cooked linguine into the skillet, ensuring it is well coated with the chickpea and artichoke mixture.

8. Adjust salt and pepper to taste. Sprinkle fresh parsley over the linguine.

9. If desired, top with grated Parmesan cheese, and serve warm.

Nutritional Information (Per Serving):

- Carbs: 68g

- Fats: 10g

- Fiber: 12g

- Protein: 15g

Pesto Zoodle Primavera

Prep Time: 15 minutes

Cook Time: 10 minutes

Servings: 2

Ingredients:

- 4 medium zucchinis, spiralized into zoodles
- 1 cup cherry tomatoes, sliced in half
- 1 bell pepper, thinly sliced
- 1 cup snap peas, trimmed and sliced
- 2 tablespoons olive oil
- ½ cup pesto sauce
- Salt and black pepper to taste
- ¼ cup pine nuts, toasted
- Grated Parmesan cheese for topping (optional)
- Fresh basil leaves for garnish (optional)

Directions:

1. Spiralize the zucchinis into zoodles and set aside.
2. In a large skillet, heat olive oil over medium heat. Add thinly sliced bell pepper and sauté until slightly softened.
3. Add cherry tomatoes and sliced snap peas to the skillet. Sauté for an additional 3-4 minutes until the vegetables are tender-crisp.
4. Add the zoodles to the skillet, tossing them with the sautéed vegetables.
5. Stir in the pesto sauce, ensuring the zoodles are well coated.
6. Cook for 2-3 minutes, allowing the zoodles to heat through without overcooking.
7. Season with salt and black pepper to taste.
8. Toast pine nuts in a dry pan over medium heat until golden brown.
9. Serve the Pesto Zoodle Primavera in bowls, topped with toasted pine nuts.
10. If desired, garnish with grated Parmesan cheese and fresh basil leaves, and serve.

Nutritional Information (Per Serving):

- Carbs: 18g
- Fats: 22g
- Fiber: 6g
- Protein: 8g

Walnut and Mushroom Bolognese Spaghetti

Prep Time: 15 minutes

Cook Time: 30 minutes

Servings: 4

Ingredients:

- 12 ounces whole wheat spaghetti
- 1 cup walnuts, finely chopped
- 2 tablespoons olive oil
- 1 onion, finely diced
- 3 cloves garlic, minced
- 8 ounces cremini mushrooms, finely chopped
- 1 carrot, grated
- 1 celery stalk, finely diced
- 1 can (28 ounces) crushed tomatoes
- 1 teaspoon dried oregano
- 1 teaspoon dried thyme
- Salt and black pepper to taste
- ¼ cup fresh parsley, chopped
- Grated Parmesan cheese for topping (optional)

Directions:

1. Cook whole wheat spaghetti according to package instructions. Drain and set aside.

2. In a large skillet, heat olive oil over medium heat. Add finely diced onion and sauté until translucent.

3. Add minced garlic to the skillet and sauté for an additional 1-2 minutes until fragrant.

4. Stir in finely chopped walnuts, finely chopped cremini mushrooms, grated carrot, and finely diced celery. Cook until the vegetables are softened.

5. Pour in crushed tomatoes and add dried oregano and dried thyme. Season with salt and black pepper to taste. Simmer for 15-20 minutes, allowing the flavors to meld.

6. While the Bolognese sauce is simmering, heat a separate pan and toast the finely chopped walnuts until fragrant and lightly browned.

7. Toss the cooked whole wheat spaghetti with the Walnut and Mushroom Bolognese sauce, ensuring it's well coated.

8. Serve in bowls, garnishing with fresh parsley and toasted walnuts.

9. Optionally, top with grated Parmesan cheese before serving.

Nutritional Information (Per Serving):

- Carbs: 57g

- Fats: 22g

- Fiber: 10g

- Protein: 14g

Roasted Red Pepper and White Bean Penne

Prep Time: 15 minutes

Cook Time: 25 minutes

Servings: 4

Ingredients:

- 12 ounces whole wheat penne pasta

- 2 red bell peppers, roasted, peeled, and sliced

- 1 can (15 ounces) white beans, drained and rinsed

- 3 tablespoons olive oil

- 2 cloves garlic, minced

- 1 teaspoon dried Italian seasoning

- Salt and black pepper to taste

- ¼ teaspoon red pepper flakes (optional)

- 1 can (14 ounces) diced tomatoes, drained

- ¼ cup fresh basil, sliced

- Grated Pecorino Romano cheese for topping (optional)

Directions:

1. Cook whole wheat penne pasta according to package instructions. Drain and set aside.

2. Roast red bell peppers until charred, then peel and slice them into thin strips.

3. In a large skillet, heat olive oil over medium heat. Add minced garlic and sauté until fragrant.

4. Add drained and rinsed white beans to the skillet, cooking for 2-3 minutes until heated through.

5. Stir in dried Italian seasoning, salt, black pepper, and red pepper flakes (if using).

6. Add the sliced roasted red peppers and drained diced tomatoes to the skillet. Cook for an additional 3-5 minutes, allowing the flavors to meld.

7. Toss the cooked whole wheat penne pasta into the skillet, ensuring it's well coated with the red pepper and white bean mixture.

8. Adjust salt and pepper to taste. Sprinkle fresh basil over the penne.

9. Serve in bowls, optionally topping with grated Pecorino Romano cheese.

Nutritional Information (Per Serving):

- Carbs: 60g

- Fats: 10g

- Fiber: 12g

- Protein: 15g

Spinach and Ricotta Stuffed Manicotti

Prep Time: 30 minutes

Cook Time: 35 minutes

Servings: 6

Ingredients:

- 12 manicotti pasta shells

- 1 tablespoon olive oil

- 1 onion, finely chopped

- 3 cloves garlic, minced

- 5 cups fresh spinach, chopped

- 2 cups ricotta cheese

- 1 cup mozzarella cheese, shredded

- ½ cup Parmesan cheese, grated

- 1 egg, beaten

- 1 teaspoon dried oregano

- 1 teaspoon dried basil

- Salt and black pepper to taste

- 2 cans (14 ounces each) crushed tomatoes

- 1 teaspoon sugar (optional)

- Fresh basil leaves for garnish (optional)

Directions:

1. Cook manicotti pasta shells according to package instructions. Drain and set aside.

2. In a large skillet, heat olive oil over medium heat. Add finely chopped onion and sauté until translucent.

3. Add minced garlic to the skillet and sauté for an additional 1-2 minutes until fragrant.

4. Stir in chopped fresh spinach and cook until wilted. Remove from heat and let it cool.

5. In a mixing bowl, add in the ricotta cheese, shredded mozzarella, grated Parmesan, beaten egg, dried oregano, dried basil, salt, and black pepper. Add the cooled spinach mixture and mix properly.

6. Preheat the oven to 350°F (175°C).

7. Stuff each cooked manicotti shell with the spinach and ricotta mixture.

8. In a separate bowl, mix crushed tomatoes with sugar (if using) and spread a thin layer on the bottom of a baking dish.

9. Arrange the stuffed manicotti in the baking dish. Cover with the remaining crushed tomato mixture.

10. Bake in the preheated oven for 25-30 minutes or until the edges are bubbly and the cheese is melted.

11. Garnish with fresh basil leaves, if desired, and serve hot.

Nutritional Information (Per Serving):

- Carbs: 42g

- Fats: 18g

- Fiber: 5g

- Protein: 22g

Lemon Garlic Edamame and Cherry Tomato Linguine

Prep Time: 15 minutes

Cook Time: 15 minutes

Servings: 4

Ingredients:

- 12 ounces whole wheat linguine

- 2 cups edamame, shelled and cooked

- 1 pint cherry tomatoes, halved

- 3 tablespoons olive oil

- 4 cloves garlic, minced

- Zest of 1 lemon

- Juice of 2 lemons

- ½ teaspoon red pepper flakes

- Salt and black pepper to taste

- ¼ cup fresh parsley, chopped

- Grated Pecorino Romano cheese for topping (optional)

Directions:

1. Cook whole wheat linguine according to package instructions. Drain and set aside.

2. In a large skillet, heat olive oil over medium heat. Add minced garlic and sauté until fragrant.

3. Add cooked edamame and halved cherry tomatoes to the skillet. Sauté for 2-3 minutes until tomatoes are slightly softened.

4. Stir in lemon zest, lemon juice, red pepper flakes, salt, and black pepper. Mix properly.

5. Add the cooked whole wheat linguine to the skillet, tossing to coat it with the lemon garlic edamame and cherry tomato mixture.

6. Cook for an additional 2-3 minutes, allowing the flavors to meld.

7. Adjust salt and pepper to taste. Sprinkle chopped fresh parsley over the linguine.

8. Optionally, top with grated Pecorino Romano cheese, and serve warm.

Nutritional Information (Per Serving):

- Carbs: 56g

- Fats: 12g

- Fiber: 12g

- Protein: 20g

Cilantro Lime Black Bean and Corn Fusilli

Prep Time: 15 minutes

Cook Time: 12 minutes

Servings: 4

Ingredients:

- 12 ounces whole wheat fusilli

- 1 can (15 ounces) black beans, drained and rinsed

- 1 cup corn kernels, fresh or frozen

- ½ red onion, finely diced

- 1 red bell pepper, diced

- ¼ cup fresh cilantro, chopped

- 2 tablespoons olive oil

- Zest of 2 limes

- Juice of 3 limes

- 1 teaspoon cumin

- Salt and black pepper to taste

- 1 avocado, sliced

- ¼ cup crumbled feta cheese (optional)

Directions:

1. Cook whole wheat fusilli according to package instructions. Drain and set aside.

2. In a large mixing bowl, add in the drained and rinsed black beans, corn kernels, finely diced red onion, diced red bell pepper, and chopped fresh cilantro, and stir to combine.

3. In a small bowl, whisk together olive oil, lime zest, lime juice, cumin, salt, and black pepper.

4. Pour the dressing over the black bean and corn mixture. Toss to combine.

5. Add the cooked whole wheat fusilli to the bowl, tossing to ensure the pasta is well coated with the cilantro lime dressing.

6. Adjust salt and pepper to taste. Gently fold in sliced avocado.

7. Serve the Cilantro Lime Black Bean and Corn Fusilli in bowls, optionally topping with crumbled feta cheese.

Nutritional Information (Per Serving):

- Carbs: 65g

- Fats: 15g

- Fiber: 15g

- Protein: 16g

Butternut Squash and Sage Farfalle

Prep Time: 20 minutes

Cook Time: 25 minutes

Servings: 4

Ingredients:

- 12 ounces farfalle pasta

- 3 cups butternut squash, peeled and diced

- 2 tablespoons olive oil

- 2 tablespoons fresh sage, chopped

- ½ cup walnuts, chopped

- ½ cup Parmesan cheese, grated

- Salt and black pepper to taste

- 1 tablespoon balsamic glaze (optional)

Directions:

1. Cook farfalle pasta according to package instructions. Drain and set aside.

2. In a large skillet, heat olive oil over medium heat. Add diced butternut squash and sauté until tender.

3. Stir in chopped fresh sage and cook for an additional 2-3 minutes to infuse the flavors.

4. Add the cooked farfalle pasta to the skillet, tossing to combine with the butternut squash and sage.

5. In a separate pan, toast the chopped walnuts until fragrant and lightly browned.

6. Sprinkle the toasted walnuts and grated Parmesan cheese over the pasta. Toss to distribute evenly.

7. Season with salt and black pepper to taste.

8. Drizzle with balsamic glaze if using.

9. Serve the Butternut Squash and Sage Farfalle in bowls, garnishing with additional fresh sage if desired.

Nutritional Information (Per Serving):

- Carbs: 60g

- Fats: 18g

- Fiber: 6g

- Protein: 12g

Tomato Basil Quinoa Mac 'n' Cheese

Prep Time: 15 minutes

Cook Time: 20 minutes

Servings: 4

Ingredients:

- 1 cup quinoa, rinsed

- 2 cups elbow macaroni

- 1 tablespoon olive oil

- 1 onion, finely diced

- 2 cloves garlic, minced

- 1 can (14 ounces) diced tomatoes

- ½ cup fresh basil, chopped

- 1 cup cheddar cheese, shredded

- ½ cup Parmesan cheese, grated

- Salt and black pepper to taste

- ½ cup breadcrumbs

- 2 tablespoons unsalted butter, melted

- Fresh basil leaves for garnish (optional)

Directions:

1. Cook quinoa according to package instructions. Set aside.

2. Cook elbow macaroni according to package instructions. Drain and set aside.

3. In a large skillet, heat olive oil over medium heat. Add finely diced onion and sauté until translucent.

4. Add minced garlic to the skillet and sauté for an additional 1-2 minutes until fragrant.

5. Stir in diced tomatoes and chopped fresh basil. Cook for 2-3 minutes, allowing the flavors to meld.

6. In a large mixing bowl, add in the cooked quinoa, cooked elbow macaroni, and the tomato basil mixture. Mix properly.

7. Add shredded cheddar cheese and grated Parmesan cheese to the bowl. Stir until the cheeses are melted and evenly distributed.

8. Season with salt and black pepper to taste.

9. In a separate bowl, add in the breadcrumbs with melted unsalted butter.

10. Preheat the oven to 375°F (190°C).

11. Transfer the quinoa mac 'n' cheese mixture to a baking dish. Top with the breadcrumb mixture.

12. Bake in the preheated oven for 15-20 minutes or until the top is golden brown and the edges are bubbly.

13. Garnish with fresh basil leaves, if desired, and serve hot.

Nutritional Information (Per Serving):

- Carbs: 57g

- Fats: 21g

- Fiber: 6g
- Protein: 18g

Spinach and Artichoke Stuffed Shells with Walnut Parmesan

Prep Time: 30 minutes

Cook Time: 30 minutes

Servings: 6

Ingredients:

- 24 jumbo pasta shells
- 2 cups frozen chopped spinach, thawed and drained
- 1 can (14 ounces) artichoke hearts, drained and finely chopped
- 1 cup ricotta cheese
- ½ cup grated Pecorino Romano cheese
- ¼ cup mayonnaise
- 2 cloves garlic, minced
- 1 teaspoon dried basil
- ½ teaspoon dried oregano
- Salt and black pepper to taste
- 1 can (28 ounces) crushed tomatoes
- 1 cup shredded mozzarella cheese
- Fresh basil leaves for garnish (optional)

Walnut Parmesan:

- 1 cup walnuts
- ¼ cup nutritional yeast
- ½ teaspoon garlic powder
- Salt to taste

Directions:

1. Cook jumbo pasta shells according to package instructions. Drain and set aside.

2. In a large mixing bowl, add in the chopped and drained frozen spinach, finely chopped artichoke hearts, ricotta cheese, grated Pecorino Romano cheese, mayonnaise, minced garlic, dried basil, dried oregano, salt, and black pepper. Mix properly.

3. Preheat the oven to 350°F (175°C).

4. Stuff each cooked pasta shell with the spinach and artichoke mixture.

5. In a blender or food processor, add in the walnuts, nutritional yeast, garlic powder, and salt. Pulse until it reaches a coarse, crumbly texture – this is your Walnut Parmesan.

6. Spread a layer of crushed tomatoes in a baking dish. Arrange the stuffed shells in the dish.

7. Top the shells with shredded mozzarella cheese and sprinkle the Walnut Parmesan over the top.

8. Bake in the preheated oven for 25-30 minutes or until the cheese is melted and bubbly.

9. Garnish with fresh basil leaves, if desired, and serve hot.

Nutritional Information (Per Serving):

- Carbs: 45g

- Fats: 21g

- Fiber: 7g

- Protein: 18g

Sundried Tomato and Basil Chickpea Penne

Prep Time: 15 minutes

Cook Time: 15 minutes

Servings: 4

Ingredients:

- 12 ounces chickpea penne pasta

- ½ cup sundried tomatoes, chopped

- 2 tablespoons olive oil

- 3 cloves garlic, minced

- 1 can (15 ounces) chickpeas, drained and rinsed

- ½ cup fresh basil, thinly sliced

- ¼ teaspoon red pepper flakes

- Salt and black pepper to taste

- ½ cup grated Pecorino Romano cheese

- ¼ cup pine nuts, toasted

- Fresh basil leaves for garnish (optional)

Directions:

1. Cook chickpea penne pasta according to package instructions. Drain and set aside.

2. In a large skillet, heat olive oil over medium heat. Add minced garlic and sauté until fragrant.

3. Add chopped sundried tomatoes to the skillet, sautéing for 2-3 minutes until softened.

4. Stir in drained and rinsed chickpeas, sliced fresh basil, red pepper flakes, salt, and black pepper. Cook for an additional 3-4 minutes.

5. Toss the cooked chickpea penne pasta into the skillet, ensuring it is well coated with the sundried tomato and chickpea mixture.

6. Adjust salt and pepper to taste. Sprinkle grated Pecorino Romano cheese over the pasta, stirring until melted and combined.

7. In a separate pan, toast the pine nuts until golden brown and fragrant.

8. Serve the Sundried Tomato and Basil Chickpea Penne in bowls, garnishing with toasted pine nuts and fresh basil leaves if desired.

Nutritional Information (Per Serving):

- Carbs: 55g

- Fats: 16g

- Fiber: 12g

- Protein: 20g

Lemon Dijon Asparagus and White Bean Linguine

Prep Time: 15 minutes

Cook Time: 15 minutes

Servings: 4

Ingredients:

- 12 ounces whole wheat linguine

- 1 bunch asparagus, trimmed and sliced

- 1 can (15 ounces) white beans, drained and rinsed

- 2 tablespoons olive oil

- Zest of 1 lemon

- Juice of 2 lemons

- 2 tablespoons Dijon mustard

- 3 cloves garlic, minced

- ½ teaspoon red pepper flakes

- Salt and black pepper to taste

- ¼ cup fresh parsley, chopped

- Grated Parmesan cheese for topping (optional)

Directions:

1. Cook whole wheat linguine according to package instructions. Drain and set aside.

2. In a large skillet, heat olive oil over medium heat. Add sliced asparagus and sauté until tender-crisp.

3. Stir in drained and rinsed white beans, minced garlic, and red pepper flakes. Cook for an additional 2-3 minutes.

4. In a small bowl, whisk together lemon zest, lemon juice, and Dijon mustard.

5. Pour the lemon-Dijon mixture over the asparagus and white beans. Mix properly.

6. Add the cooked whole wheat linguine to the skillet, tossing to coat it with the asparagus and white bean mixture.

7. Season with salt and black pepper to taste. Sprinkle chopped fresh parsley over the linguine.

8. If desired, top with grated Parmesan cheese before serving.

Nutritional Information (Per Serving):

- Carbs: 54g

- Fats: 10g

- Fiber: 12g

- Protein: 16g

Butternut Squash and Sage Gnocchi with Almond Cream Sauce

Prep Time: 30 minutes

Cook Time: 25 minutes

Servings: 4

Ingredients:

For the Gnocchi:

- 2 cups butternut squash, peeled and diced
- 2 cups potatoes, peeled and diced
- 2 cups all-purpose flour
- Salt to taste
- 1 teaspoon dried sage

For the Almond Cream Sauce:

- 1 cup almond milk
- ½ cup raw almonds
- 2 tablespoons nutritional yeast
- 2 cloves garlic, minced
- 2 tablespoons olive oil
- Salt and black pepper to taste

Additional Ingredients:

- Fresh sage leaves for garnish (optional)
- Grated vegan Parmesan cheese for topping (optional)

Directions:

For the Gnocchi:

1. Boil the diced butternut squash and potatoes until tender. Drain and let them cool slightly.
2. In a large mixing bowl, mash the butternut squash and potatoes until smooth.
3. Add all-purpose flour, salt, and dried sage to the mashed mixture. Knead the dough until properly combined.
4. Divide the dough into portions and roll each portion into a rope.

5. Cut the ropes into bite-sized pieces to form the gnocchi.

6. Bring a large pot of salted water to a boil. Cook the gnocchi in batches until they float to the surface. Remove with a slotted spoon and set aside.

For the Almond Cream Sauce:

1. In a blender, add in the almond milk, raw almonds, nutritional yeast, minced garlic, olive oil, salt, and black pepper. Blend until smooth.

Assembling the Dish:

1. In a large skillet, heat the almond cream sauce over medium heat.

2. Add the cooked gnocchi to the skillet, tossing to coat them with the almond cream sauce.

3. Cook for an additional 2-3 minutes until the gnocchi are heated through.

4. Garnish with fresh sage leaves if desired.

5. Optionally, top with grated vegan Parmesan cheese before serving.

Nutritional Information (Per Serving):

- Carbs: 75g

- Fats: 25g

- Fiber: 10g

- Protein: 15g

Pesto Zoodle Caprese Salad with Balsamic Drizzle

Prep Time: 20 minutes

Cook Time: 0 minutes

Servings: 4

Ingredients:

- 4 medium zucchinis, spiralized into zoodles

- 1 cup cherry tomatoes, halved

- 1 cup fresh mozzarella balls (bocconcini), halved

- ½ cup fresh basil leaves, thinly sliced

- ¼ cup pine nuts, toasted

- Salt and black pepper to taste

For the Pesto:

- 2 cups fresh basil leaves

- ½ cup grated Parmesan cheese

- ⅓ cup pine nuts

- 2 cloves garlic, minced

- ½ cup olive oil

- Salt and black pepper to taste

For the Balsamic Drizzle:

- ¼ cup balsamic glaze

Directions:

For the Pesto:

1. In a food processor, add in the fresh basil leaves, grated Parmesan cheese, pine nuts, and minced garlic.

2. Pulse until the ingredients are finely chopped.

3. With the food processor running, slowly pour in the olive oil until the pesto reaches a smooth consistency.

4. Season with salt and black pepper to taste. Set aside.

For the Salad:

1. Spiralize the zucchinis into zoodles using a spiralizer.

2. In a large mixing bowl, add in the zoodles, halved cherry tomatoes, halved fresh mozzarella balls, and thinly sliced fresh basil leaves.

3. Add the toasted pine nuts to the bowl.

4. Pour the prepared pesto over the salad and toss until all ingredients are well coated.

5. Season with salt and black pepper to taste.

Serving:

1. Divide the Pesto Zoodle Caprese Salad among plates.

2. Drizzle balsamic glaze over each serving.

3. Optionally, garnish with additional fresh basil leaves, and serve at room temperature.

Nutritional Information (Per Serving):

- Carbs: 15g

- Fats: 28g

- Fiber: 4g

- Protein: 10g

Chapter 7: Seafood Alternatives

Almond Crusted Tofu "Fish" and Chips

Prep Time: 20 minutes
Cook Time: 25 minutes
Servings: 4

Ingredients:

- 1 block (14 ounces) extra-firm tofu, pressed and sliced into "fish" fillets

- 1 cup almond meal

- 1 cup panko breadcrumbs

- 2 teaspoons dried dill

- 1 teaspoon garlic powder

- 1 teaspoon onion powder

- ½ teaspoon paprika

- ½ teaspoon salt

- ¼ teaspoon black pepper

- 1 cup all-purpose flour

- 2 flax eggs (2 tablespoons ground flaxseeds mixed with 6 tablespoons water)

- 1 cup unsweetened almond milk

- 1 cup cornstarch (for coating tofu)

- 4 large potatoes, cut into thick fries

- Vegetable oil (for frying)

Directions:

1. **Preheat Oven:** Preheat the oven to 425°F (220°C).

2. **Prepare "Fish" Fillets:** In a shallow dish, add in the almond meal, panko breadcrumbs, dried dill, garlic powder, onion powder, paprika, salt, and black pepper. Set aside.

3. **Coat Tofu:** Coat each tofu fillet in flour, dip into the flax egg mixture, and then coat with the almond meal mixture. Ensure each fillet is evenly coated.

4. **Bake "Fish" Fillets:** Place the coated tofu fillets on a baking sheet lined with parchment paper. Bake for 20-25 minutes or until the coating is golden and crispy.

5. **Prepare Batter:** In a bowl, whisk together flour, almond milk, and a pinch of salt to make a smooth batter.

6. **Coat Potato Fries:** Toss the potato fries in cornstarch until evenly coated. Dip each fry into the batter, allowing excess to drip off.

7. **Fry Potato Fries:** Heat vegetable oil in a deep pan to 350°F (175°C). Fry the coated potato fries until golden brown and crispy. Remove and place on a paper towel to absorb excess oil.

8. **Serve:** Serve the almond-crusted tofu "fish" fillets with the crispy potato fries.

Nutritional Information (Per Serving):

- **Carbs:** 45g

- **Fats:** 18g

- **Fiber:** 7g

- **Protein:** 15g

Seared Tempeh "Scallops" with Lemon Butter Sauce
Prep Time: 15 minutes
Cook Time: 15 minutes
Servings: 4

Ingredients:

- 2 packages (8 ounces each) tempeh, cut into "scallops"

- ¼ cup soy sauce

- 1 tablespoon olive oil

- 1 teaspoon garlic powder

- ½ teaspoon smoked paprika

- ¼ teaspoon black pepper

- 2 tablespoons vegetable oil (for searing)

- ½ cup vegetable broth

- 2 tablespoons unsalted butter

- Juice of 1 lemon

- 2 tablespoons chopped fresh parsley

- Salt, to taste

Directions:

1. **Marinate Tempeh:** In a bowl, mix tempeh "scallops" with soy sauce, olive oil, garlic powder, smoked paprika, and black pepper. Let it marinate for at least 10 minutes.

2. **Sear Tempeh:** Heat vegetable oil in a skillet over medium-high heat. Sear the marinated tempeh "scallops" for 2-3 minutes on each side until golden brown. Remove from the skillet and set aside.

3. **Prepare Lemon Butter Sauce:** In the same skillet, add vegetable broth, butter, and lemon juice. Stir and simmer for 2-3 minutes until the sauce thickens slightly.

4. **Finish Tempeh:** Return the seared tempeh "scallops" to the skillet. Coat them in the lemon butter sauce and cook for an additional 2 minutes until heated through. Season with salt to taste.

5. **Serve:** Plate the seared tempeh "scallops" and drizzle with the lemon butter sauce. Garnish with chopped fresh parsley.

Nutritional Information (Per Serving):

- **Carbs:** 12g

- **Fats:** 16g

- **Fiber:** 5g

- **Protein:** 22g

Cajun Spiced Chickpea Cakes with Remoulade

Prep Time: 20 minutes
Cook Time: 15 minutes
Servings: 4

Ingredients:

For Chickpea Cakes:

- 2 cans (15 ounces each) chickpeas, drained and rinsed

- ½ cup breadcrumbs

- ¼ cup diced red bell pepper

- ¼ cup diced green onions

- 2 cloves garlic, minced

- 1 teaspoon Cajun seasoning

- ½ teaspoon smoked paprika

- ¼ teaspoon cayenne pepper

- 2 tablespoons olive oil (for cooking)

For Remoulade:

- ½ cup mayonnaise

- 2 tablespoons Dijon mustard

- 1 tablespoon capers, chopped

- 1 tablespoon fresh parsley, chopped

- 1 teaspoon hot sauce

- 1 teaspoon lemon juice

- Salt and black pepper, to taste

Directions:

1. **Prepare Chickpea Mixture:** In a food processor, add in the chickpeas, breadcrumbs, red bell pepper, green onions, garlic, Cajun seasoning, smoked paprika, and cayenne pepper. Pulse until properly combined but still slightly chunky.

2. **Form Chickpea Cakes:** Divide the chickpea mixture into 8 portions and shape them into patties.

3. **Cook Chickpea Cakes:** Heat olive oil in a skillet over medium heat. Cook the chickpea cakes for 3-4 minutes on each side or until golden brown.

4. **Make Remoulade Sauce:** In a bowl, mix mayonnaise, Dijon mustard, capers, parsley, hot sauce, lemon juice, salt, and black pepper to make the remoulade sauce.

5. **Serve:** Plate the Cajun spiced chickpea cakes and drizzle with remoulade sauce.

Nutritional Information (Per Serving):

- **Carbs:** 35g

- **Fats:** 18g

- **Fiber:** 9g

- **Protein:** 12g

Teriyaki Glazed Eggplant "Eel" Sushi Bowl

Prep Time: 15 minutes
Cook Time: 20 minutes
Servings: 4

Ingredients:

For Teriyaki Glazed Eggplant:

- 2 large eggplants, sliced into thin strips
- ¼ cup soy sauce
- 2 tablespoons mirin
- 2 tablespoons rice vinegar
- 2 tablespoons brown sugar
- 1 tablespoon sesame oil
- 1 teaspoon grated ginger
- 1 teaspoon cornstarch dissolved in 2 teaspoons water

For Sushi Bowl:

- 2 cups cooked sushi rice
- 1 avocado, sliced
- 1 cucumber, julienned
- 1 carrot, julienned
- 4 sheets nori, toasted and cut into strips
- Sesame seeds, for garnish
- Green onions, sliced, for garnish

Directions:

1. **Prepare Teriyaki Glazed Eggplant:** In a bowl, whisk together soy sauce, mirin, rice vinegar, brown sugar, sesame oil, and grated ginger. Set aside.

2. **Cook Eggplant Strips:** Heat a pan over medium heat and add the eggplant strips. Pour the teriyaki sauce over the eggplant and cook for 10-12 minutes, stirring occasionally, until the eggplant is tender.

3. **Thicken Sauce:** Add the cornstarch-water mixture to the pan and stir until the sauce thickens. Remove from heat.

4. **Assemble Sushi Bowl:** Divide the sushi rice among four bowls. Top with teriyaki glazed eggplant strips, avocado slices, julienned cucumber, julienned carrot, and nori strips.

5. **Garnish and Serve:** Sprinkle sesame seeds and sliced green onions over the sushi bowls. Serve immediately.

Nutritional Information (Per Serving):

- **Carbs:** 65g

- **Fats:** 10g

- **Fiber:** 10g

- **Protein:** 6g

Artichoke and Hearts of Palm "Crab" Cakes

Prep Time: 20 minutes
Cook Time: 15 minutes
Servings: 4

Ingredients:

- 1 can (14 ounces) artichoke hearts, drained and finely chopped

- 1 can (14 ounces) hearts of palm, drained and finely chopped

- ½ cup breadcrumbs

- ¼ cup mayonnaise

- 2 tablespoons Dijon mustard

- 1 tablespoon Old Bay seasoning

- 1 teaspoon lemon zest

- ¼ cup chopped fresh parsley

- Salt and black pepper, to taste

- 2 tablespoons olive oil (for cooking)

Directions:

1. **Prepare Mixture:** In a bowl, add in the chopped artichoke hearts, chopped hearts of palm, breadcrumbs, mayonnaise, Dijon mustard, Old Bay seasoning, lemon zest, chopped parsley, salt, and black pepper. Mix until properly combined.

2. **Form "Crab" Cakes:** Divide the mixture into 8 portions and shape them into patties.

3. **Cook "Crab" Cakes:** Heat olive oil in a skillet over medium heat. Cook the "crab" cakes for 3-4 minutes on each side or until golden brown.

4. **Serve:** Plate the artichoke and hearts of palm "crab" cakes.

Nutritional Information (Per Serving):

- **Carbs:** 18g

- **Fats:** 12g

- **Fiber:** 6g

- **Protein:** 4g

Lemon Dill Quinoa Stuffed Bell Peppers with "Shrimp"

Prep Time: 20 minutes
Cook Time: 30 minutes
Servings: 4

Ingredients:

- 4 large bell peppers, halved and seeds removed

- 1 cup quinoa, cooked

- 1 pound flexitarian shrimp, peeled and deveined

- 1 tablespoon olive oil

- 1 onion, finely diced

- 2 cloves garlic, minced

- 1 cup cherry tomatoes, diced

- ¼ cup fresh dill, chopped

- Zest of 1 lemon

- Juice of 1 lemon

- Salt and black pepper, to taste

- ½ cup feta cheese, crumbled (optional, for garnish)

Directions:

1. **Preheat Oven:** Preheat the oven to 375°F (190°C).

2. **Prepare Bell Peppers:** Place the halved bell peppers in a baking dish.

3. **Cook Quinoa:** In a pot, cook the quinoa according to package instructions.

4. **Cook "Shrimp":** In a skillet, heat olive oil over medium heat. Add flexitarian shrimp and cook until opaque, about 2-3 minutes per side. Remove from the skillet and set aside.

5. **Sauté Onion and Garlic:** In the same skillet, sauté diced onion and minced garlic until softened.

6. **Combine Ingredients:** Put the cooked quinoa, flexitarian shrimp, sautéed onion and garlic, diced cherry tomatoes, chopped fresh dill, lemon zest, and lemon juice into a large bowl and stir to combine. Season with salt and black pepper.

7. **Stuff Bell Peppers:** Spoon the quinoa mixture into the halved bell peppers.

8. **Bake:** Cover the baking dish with foil and bake in the preheated oven for 20-25 minutes or until the bell peppers are tender.

9. **Garnish and Serve:** Garnish with crumbled feta cheese if desired. Serve the stuffed bell peppers warm.

Nutritional Information (Per Serving):

- **Carbs:** 45g

- **Fats:** 10g

- **Fiber:** 9g

- **Protein:** 20g

Coconut-Curry Seitan "Shrimp" Stir-Fry

Prep Time: 15 minutes
Cook Time: 15 minutes
Servings: 4

Ingredients:

- 1 pound flexitarian seitan "shrimp"

- 2 tablespoons coconut oil

- 1 onion, thinly sliced

- 1 bell pepper, thinly sliced

- 1 carrot, julienned

- 1 cup snap peas, ends trimmed

- 3 cloves garlic, minced

- 1 tablespoon fresh ginger, grated

- 1 can (14 ounces) coconut milk

- 2 tablespoons red curry paste

- 2 tablespoons soy sauce

- 1 tablespoon maple syrup

- Juice of 1 lime

- Fresh cilantro, for garnish

- Cooked rice or noodles, for serving

Directions:

1. **Prepare "Shrimp":** If using frozen flexitarian seitan "shrimp," thaw according to package instructions.

2. **Stir-Fry Vegetables:** In a large wok or skillet, heat coconut oil over medium-high heat. Add sliced onion, bell pepper, julienned carrot, and snap peas. Stir-fry for 3-4 minutes until vegetables are tender-crisp.

3. **Add "Shrimp":** Add flexitarian seitan "shrimp" to the vegetables and cook for an additional 2-3 minutes, stirring occasionally.

4. **Make Coconut-Curry Sauce:** Push the vegetables and "shrimp" to one side of the wok. On the other side, add minced garlic and grated ginger. Sauté for about 1 minute until fragrant. Mix in coconut milk, red curry paste, soy sauce, maple syrup, and lime juice. Stir until properly combined.

5. **Combine the Ingredients and Simmer:** Mix the vegetables, "shrimp," and sauce together. Allow the mixture to simmer for 5-7 minutes, allowing the flavors to meld and the sauce to thicken.

6. **Serve:** Serve the Coconut-Curry Seitan "Shrimp" Stir-Fry over cooked rice or noodles. Garnish with fresh cilantro.

Nutritional Information (Per Serving):

- **Carbs:** 35g

- **Fats:** 15g

- **Fiber:** 7g

- **Protein:** 20g

Blackened Jackfruit "Tuna" Salad Wraps

Prep Time: 20 minutes
Cook Time: 10 minutes
Servings: 4

Ingredients:

For Blackened Jackfruit "Tuna" Salad:

- 2 cans (20 ounces total) young green jackfruit in water, drained and shredded
- 2 tablespoons olive oil
- 1 tablespoon blackened seasoning
- 1 teaspoon smoked paprika
- ½ teaspoon garlic powder
- ½ teaspoon onion powder
- Salt and black pepper, to taste
- ¼ cup vegan mayonnaise
- 2 tablespoons Dijon mustard
- 1 celery stalk, finely diced
- ¼ red onion, finely diced
- 1 tablespoon fresh dill, chopped
- Juice of 1 lemon

For Wraps:

- 4 large whole-grain or gluten-free tortillas
- Spinach or lettuce leaves, for wrapping
- Avocado slices, for garnish

Directions:

1. **Prepare Jackfruit "Tuna" Salad:** In a skillet, heat olive oil over medium heat. Add shredded jackfruit, blackened seasoning, smoked paprika, garlic powder, onion powder, salt, and black pepper. Sauté for 5-7 minutes until jackfruit is well-coated and slightly crispy.

2. **Make "Tuna" Salad Mixture:** In a large bowl, add in the sautéed jackfruit with vegan mayonnaise, Dijon mustard, diced celery, diced red onion, chopped fresh dill, and lemon juice. Mix until properly combined.

3. **Assemble Wraps:** Lay out the tortillas and place spinach or lettuce leaves on each one. Spoon the blackened jackfruit "tuna" salad mixture onto the center of each tortilla.

4. **Garnish and Wrap:** Top with avocado slices. Fold the sides of the tortilla in, then fold the bottom and roll to create a wrap.

5. **Serve:** Serve the Blackened Jackfruit "Tuna" Salad Wraps immediately.

Nutritional Information (Per Serving):

- **Carbs:** 45g

- **Fats:** 15g

- **Fiber:** 10g

- **Protein:** 10g

Mediterranean Stuffed Zucchini with "Feta" and "Shrimp"

Prep Time: 25 minutes
Cook Time: 25 minutes
Servings: 4

Ingredients:

For Stuffed Zucchini:

- 4 large zucchinis, halved lengthwise

- 1 pound flexitarian shrimp, peeled and deveined

- 2 tablespoons olive oil

- 1 onion, finely diced

- 3 cloves garlic, minced

- 1 cup cherry tomatoes, diced

- ½ cup Kalamata olives, sliced

- ¼ cup fresh parsley, chopped

- Salt and black pepper, to taste

For "Feta" Mixture:

- 1 cup crumbled vegan feta cheese

- 1 tablespoon olive oil

- 1 teaspoon dried oregano

- 1 teaspoon lemon zest

- Juice of 1 lemon

Directions:

1. **Preheat Oven:** Preheat the oven to 375°F (190°C).

2. **Prepare Zucchinis:** Scoop out the flesh from the halved zucchinis, leaving a shell. Chop the zucchini flesh finely and set aside.

3. **Cook "Shrimp":** In a skillet, heat olive oil over medium heat. Add flexitarian shrimp and cook until opaque, about 2-3 minutes per side. Remove from the skillet and set aside.

4. **Sauté Onion and Garlic:** In the same skillet, sauté diced onion and minced garlic until softened.

5. **Prepare Filling:** Add the chopped zucchini flesh, diced cherry tomatoes, sliced Kalamata olives, and flexitarian shrimp to the skillet. Sauté for 3-4 minutes until the mixture is properly combined. Season with salt and black pepper.

6. **Make "Feta" Mixture:** In a bowl, add in the crumbled vegan feta cheese, olive oil, dried oregano, lemon zest, and lemon juice and stir to combine.

7. **Combine Filling and "Feta":** Remove the skillet from heat. Mix the sautéed filling with the "feta" mixture. Stir in chopped fresh parsley.

8. **Stuff Zucchinis:** Fill each zucchini half with the mixture.

9. **Bake:** Place the stuffed zucchinis in a baking dish and bake in the preheated oven for 20-25 minutes or until the zucchinis are tender.

10. **Serve:** Serve the Mediterranean Stuffed Zucchini with flexitarian "shrimp" and "feta" immediately.

Nutritional Information (Per Serving):

- **Carbs:** 20g

- **Fats:** 12g

- **Fiber:** 6g

Spicy Mango Glazed Jackfruit "Shrimp" Lettuce Wraps

Prep Time: 20 minutes
Cook Time: 15 minutes
Servings: 4

Ingredients:

For Spicy Mango Glazed Jackfruit "Shrimp":

- 1 pound flexitarian jackfruit "shrimp," peeled and deveined

- 2 tablespoons olive oil

- ¼ cup mango puree

- 2 tablespoons soy sauce

- 1 tablespoon sriracha sauce

- 1 tablespoon maple syrup

- 1 teaspoon grated ginger

- 2 cloves garlic, minced

- 1 teaspoon cornstarch dissolved in 2 teaspoons water

For Lettuce Wraps:

- 1 head iceberg lettuce, leaves separated

- 1 cup cucumber, julienned

- 1 cup carrots, julienned

- ¼ cup fresh cilantro, chopped

- Sesame seeds, for garnish

Directions:

1. **Cook Flexitarian "Shrimp":** In a skillet, heat olive oil over medium heat. Add flexitarian jackfruit "shrimp" and cook until opaque, about 2-3 minutes per side.

2. **Prepare Glaze:** In a bowl, mix mango puree, soy sauce, sriracha sauce, maple syrup, grated ginger, and minced garlic. Pour the glaze over the cooked "shrimp."

3. **Thicken Glaze:** In a small bowl, dissolve cornstarch in water. Add it to the skillet with the "shrimp" and glaze. Stir until the sauce thickens and coats the "shrimp."

4. **Assemble Lettuce Wraps:** Place a spoonful of the spicy mango glazed "shrimp" in each lettuce leaf. Top with julienned cucumber, julienned carrots, and chopped fresh cilantro.

5. **Garnish and Serve:** Sprinkle sesame seeds over the lettuce wraps. Serve the Spicy Mango Glazed Jackfruit "Shrimp" Lettuce Wraps immediately.

Nutritional Information (Per Serving):

- **Carbs:** 15g

- **Fats:** 8g

- **Fiber:** 5g

- **Protein:** 10g

Smoked Paprika Seitan "Scallops" with Garlic Aioli

Prep Time: 15 minutes
Cook Time: 10 minutes
Servings: 4

Ingredients:

For Smoked Paprika Seitan "Scallops":

- 1 pound flexitarian seitan strips

- 2 tablespoons olive oil

- 1 teaspoon smoked paprika

- ½ teaspoon garlic powder

- ½ teaspoon onion powder

- Salt and black pepper, to taste

- 1 tablespoon fresh parsley, chopped (for garnish)

For Garlic Aioli:

- ½ cup vegan mayonnaise

- 2 cloves garlic, minced

- 1 tablespoon lemon juice

- Salt and black pepper, to taste

Directions:

1. **Prepare Smoked Paprika Seitan "Scallops":** In a bowl, toss flexitarian seitan strips with olive oil, smoked paprika, garlic powder, onion powder, salt, and black pepper.

2. **Sauté "Scallops":** In a skillet, heat olive oil over medium-high heat. Add the seasoned seitan strips and sauté for 3-4 minutes until golden brown.

3. **Make Garlic Aioli:** In a small bowl, mix vegan mayonnaise, minced garlic, lemon juice, salt, and black pepper to create the garlic aioli.

4. **Serve:** Plate the smoked paprika seitan "scallops" and drizzle with garlic aioli. Garnish with chopped fresh parsley.

Nutritional Information (Per Serving):

- **Carbs:** 10g

- **Fats:** 12g

- **Fiber:** 2g

- **Protein:** 20g

Lemon Herb Grilled Tofu "Fish" Tacos

Prep Time: 30 minutes
Cook Time: 10 minutes
Servings: 4

Ingredients:

For Lemon Herb Grilled Tofu "Fish":

- 1 block (14 ounces) extra-firm tofu, pressed and sliced into "fish" fillets

- 2 tablespoons olive oil

- 2 tablespoons lemon juice

- 1 teaspoon lemon zest

- 1 teaspoon dried oregano

- 1 teaspoon dried thyme

- 1 teaspoon smoked paprika

- Salt and black pepper, to taste

For Tacos:

- 8 small corn or flour tortillas

- 1 cup shredded cabbage

- 1 avocado, sliced

- ½ cup cherry tomatoes, diced

- Fresh cilantro, for garnish

- Lime wedges, for serving

Directions:

1. **Marinate Tofu "Fish":** In a bowl, whisk together olive oil, lemon juice, lemon zest, dried oregano, dried thyme, smoked paprika, salt, and black pepper. Place tofu "fish" fillets in the marinade, ensuring they are well-coated. Marinate for at least 20 minutes.

2. **Grill Tofu "Fish":** Preheat a grill or grill pan over medium-high heat. Grill the marinated tofu "fish" for 3-4 minutes on each side until grill marks appear, and the tofu is heated through.

3. **Warm Tortillas:** Heat the tortillas according to package instructions.

4. **Assemble Tacos:** Place a couple of tofu "fish" fillets on each tortilla. Top with shredded cabbage, sliced avocado, diced cherry tomatoes, and garnish with fresh cilantro.

5. **Serve:** Serve the Lemon Herb Grilled Tofu "Fish" Tacos with lime wedges on the side.

Nutritional Information (Per Serving):

- **Carbs:** 30g

- **Fats:** 14g

- **Fiber:** 8g

- **Protein:** 10g

Coconut Curry Cauliflower "Crab" Soup

Prep Time: 15 minutes
Cook Time: 25 minutes
Servings: 4

Ingredients:

- 1 tablespoon olive oil

- 1 onion, diced

- 3 cloves garlic, minced

- 1 tablespoon ginger, grated

- 1 head cauliflower, chopped into florets

- 1 can (14 ounces) chickpeas, drained and rinsed

- 1 can (14 ounces) coconut milk

- 4 cups vegetable broth

- 2 tablespoons red curry paste

- 1 tablespoon soy sauce

- 1 tablespoon lime juice

- 1 tablespoon brown sugar

- 1 cup flexitarian crab meat

- Salt and black pepper, to taste

- Fresh cilantro, for garnish

Directions:

1. **Sauté Aromatics:** In a large pot, heat olive oil over medium heat. Add diced onion, minced garlic, and grated ginger. Sauté until the onion is translucent.

2. **Add Cauliflower and Chickpeas:** Add chopped cauliflower florets and drained chickpeas to the pot. Cook for 5 minutes, stirring occasionally.

3. **Make Coconut Curry Base:** Pour in coconut milk, vegetable broth, red curry paste, soy sauce, lime juice, and brown sugar. Stir to combine.

4. **Simmer:** Bring the soup to a simmer and let it cook for 15-20 minutes or until the cauliflower is tender.

5. **Blend Soup:** Use an immersion blender to blend the soup until smooth. Alternatively, transfer the soup to a blender in batches, blend, and return to the pot.

6. **Add Flexitarian Crab Meat:** Stir in flexitarian crab meat and cook for an additional 5 minutes until heated through.

7. **Season and Garnish:** Season the soup with salt and black pepper to taste. Garnish with fresh cilantro.

8. **Serve:** Ladle the Coconut Curry Cauliflower "Crab" Soup into bowls and serve hot.

Nutritional Information (Per Serving):

- **Carbs:** 35g

- **Fats:** 20g

- **Fiber:** 10g

- **Protein:** 10g

Crispy Teriyaki Tempeh "Tuna" Poke Bowl
Prep Time: 30 minutes
Cook Time: 15 minutes
Servings: 4

Ingredients:

For Crispy Teriyaki Tempeh "Tuna":

- 2 packages (16 ounces total) flexitarian tempeh, diced
- ¼ cup soy sauce
- 2 tablespoons mirin
- 1 tablespoon rice vinegar
- 1 tablespoon maple syrup
- 1 tablespoon sesame oil
- 1 tablespoon cornstarch
- 2 tablespoons vegetable oil (for frying)

For Poke Bowl:

- 2 cups sushi rice, cooked
- 1 cucumber, diced
- 1 avocado, sliced
- 1 cup edamame, steamed
- ¼ cup pickled ginger
- 2 tablespoons sesame seeds
- 4 green onions, sliced

Directions:

1. **Prepare Teriyaki Tempeh "Tuna":** In a bowl, add in the diced flexitarian tempeh with soy sauce, mirin, rice vinegar, maple syrup, sesame oil, and cornstarch and stir to combine. Allow it to marinate for at least 15 minutes.

2. **Sauté Tempeh:** In a skillet, heat vegetable oil over medium-high heat. Add the marinated tempeh and sauté for 5-7 minutes until crispy and golden brown.

3. **Assemble Poke Bowl:** In serving bowls, arrange cooked sushi rice. Top with crispy teriyaki tempeh "tuna," diced cucumber, sliced avocado, steamed edamame, pickled ginger, sesame seeds, and sliced green onions.

4. **Serve:** Serve the Crispy Teriyaki Tempeh "Tuna" Poke Bowl immediately.

Nutritional Information (Per Serving):

- **Carbs:** 60g

- **Fats:** 20g
- **Fiber:** 12g
- **Protein:** 25g

Chapter 8: Grain-Free Delights

Spaghetti Squash Pad Thai with Tofu

Prep Time: 20 minutes

Cook Time: 40 minutes

Servings: 4

Ingredients:

- 1 medium-sized spaghetti squash, halved and seeds removed
- 14-ounce extra-firm tofu, pressed and cubed
- 2 carrots, julienned
- 1 red bell pepper, thinly sliced
- 1 cup snap peas, ends trimmed
- 3 green onions, sliced
- 3 cloves garlic, minced
- ½ cup unsalted peanuts, chopped
- 2 eggs, beaten
- 3 tablespoons avocado oil

For the Sauce:

- ¼ cup soy sauce
- 3 tablespoons hoisin sauce
- 2 tablespoons rice vinegar
- 1 tablespoon maple syrup
- 1 teaspoon sriracha sauce (adjust to taste)

Directions:

1. Preheat the oven to 400°F (200°C).

2. Place the spaghetti squash halves on a baking sheet, cut side up. Drizzle with 1 tablespoon of avocado oil and season with salt and pepper. Roast in the oven for 35-40 minutes or until the squash is tender. Once cooked, use a fork to scrape out the strands into a bowl and set aside.

3. In a small bowl, whisk together all the sauce ingredients - soy sauce, hoisin sauce, rice vinegar, maple syrup, and sriracha. Set aside.

4. In a large skillet or wok, heat 2 tablespoons of avocado oil over medium heat. Add the cubed tofu and cook until golden brown on all sides. Remove tofu from the skillet and set aside.

5. In the same skillet, add the remaining tablespoon of oil. Add garlic, sliced bell pepper, julienned carrots, and snap peas. Stir-fry for 3-4 minutes or until the vegetables are tender-crisp.

6. Push the vegetables to one side of the skillet and pour the beaten eggs into the other side. Scramble the eggs and cook until just set.

7. Add the cooked spaghetti squash, tofu, and the prepared sauce to the skillet. Toss everything together until properly combined and heated through.

8. Stir in sliced green onions and chopped peanuts. Cook for an additional 2 minutes.

Nutritional Information (Per Serving):

- Carbs: 45g

- Fats: 20g

- Fiber: 10g

- Protein: 18g

Cauliflower and Chickpea Crust Pizza

Prep Time: 15 minutes

Cook Time: 30 minutes

Servings: 4

Ingredients:

For the Crust:

- 1 small cauliflower head, riced

- 1 cup chickpea flour

- ½ cup grated Parmesan cheese

- 2 large eggs

- 1 teaspoon dried oregano

- 1 teaspoon garlic powder

- ½ teaspoon salt

- ¼ teaspoon black pepper

For the Toppings:

- ½ cup tomato sauce

- 1 cup shredded mozzarella cheese

- ½ cup cherry tomatoes, sliced

- ¼ cup red onion, thinly sliced

- ¼ cup black olives, sliced

- Fresh basil leaves, for garnish

Directions:

1. Preheat the oven to 425°F (220°C).

2. Place the riced cauliflower in a clean kitchen towel and squeeze out excess moisture. Transfer the cauliflower to a mixing bowl.

3. Add chickpea flour, grated Parmesan cheese, eggs, dried oregano, garlic powder, salt, and black pepper to the cauliflower. Mix until properly combined to form the pizza crust dough.

4. Line a baking sheet with parchment paper. Transfer the dough onto the prepared baking sheet and spread it out into a thin, even layer to form the pizza crust.

5. Bake the crust in the preheated oven for 15-20 minutes or until golden brown and set.

6. Remove the crust from the oven and spread tomato sauce evenly over the surface. Sprinkle shredded mozzarella cheese, sliced cherry tomatoes, red onion, and black olives on top.

7. Return the pizza to the oven and bake for an additional 10 minutes or until the cheese is melted and bubbly.

8. Garnish the pizza with fresh basil leaves before serving.

Nutritional Information (Per Serving):

- Carbs: 30g

- Fats: 15g

- Fiber: 8g

- Protein: 20g

Zucchini Lasagna with Cashew Ricotta

Prep Time: 30 minutes

Cook Time: 45 minutes

Servings: 6

Ingredients:

For the Cashew Ricotta:

- 1 cup raw cashews, soaked in water for 4 hours
- 2 cloves garlic, minced
- 2 tablespoons nutritional yeast
- 2 tablespoons lemon juice
- ½ teaspoon salt
- ¼ cup water (for blending)

For the Lasagna:

- 4 large zucchinis, sliced lengthwise
- 1 tablespoon olive oil
- 1 onion, diced
- 2 cloves garlic, minced
- 1 pound ground turkey (flexitarian option) or plant-based ground meat
- 1 can (28 ounces) crushed tomatoes
- 1 can (14 ounces) diced tomatoes
- 1 teaspoon dried oregano
- 1 teaspoon dried basil
- Salt and black pepper to taste
- 2 cups spinach, chopped
- 2 cups shredded mozzarella cheese

Directions:

For the Cashew Ricotta:

1. In a blender, add in the soaked cashews, minced garlic, nutritional yeast, lemon juice, salt, and water.

2. Blend until smooth and creamy, adding more water if needed. Set aside.

For the Lasagna:

1. Preheat the oven to 375°F (190°C).

2. Heat olive oil in a large skillet over medium heat. Add diced onions and minced garlic, sautéing until softened.

3. Add ground turkey (or plant-based meat) to the skillet, breaking it up with a spoon. Cook until browned.

4. Stir in crushed tomatoes, diced tomatoes, dried oregano, dried basil, salt, and black pepper. Simmer for 15-20 minutes.

5. In a separate pan, lightly grill the zucchini slices until they are just tender. Set aside.

6. In a baking dish, layer zucchini slices, followed by a portion of the tomato and meat sauce, chopped spinach, and cashew ricotta. Repeat the layers.

7. Top the lasagna with shredded mozzarella cheese.

8. Bake in the preheated oven for 25-30 minutes or until the cheese is melted and bubbly.

Nutritional Information (Per Serving):

- Carbs: 20g

- Fats: 15g

- Fiber: 5g

- Protein: 25g

Portobello Mushroom Cap Burgers with Guacamole

Prep Time: 15 minutes

Cook Time: 15 minutes

Servings: 4

Ingredients:

For the Mushroom Caps:

- 4 large Portobello mushroom caps, cleaned and stems removed

- 2 tablespoons balsamic vinegar

- 2 tablespoons olive oil

- 2 cloves garlic, minced

- Salt and black pepper to taste

For the Guacamole:

- 2 ripe avocados, peeled and mashed

- 1 tomato, diced

- ¼ red onion, finely chopped

- ¼ cup fresh cilantro, chopped

- 1 lime, juiced

- Salt and black pepper to taste

For Assembling:

- 4 whole-grain burger buns

- 4 lettuce leaves

- 4 slices of tomato

- 4 slices of red onion

Directions:

For the Mushroom Caps:

1. In a small bowl, whisk together balsamic vinegar, olive oil, minced garlic, salt, and black pepper.

2. Place the Portobello mushroom caps in a shallow dish and brush both sides with the balsamic mixture. Let them marinate for at least 10 minutes.

3. Preheat the grill or grill pan over medium-high heat. Grill the mushroom caps for 5-7 minutes per side or until tender.

For the Guacamole:

1. In a medium bowl, add in the mashed avocados, diced tomato, chopped red onion, chopped cilantro, lime juice, salt, and black pepper. Mix properly.

For Assembling:

1. Toast the whole-grain burger buns on the grill or in a toaster.

2. Assemble the burgers by placing a grilled Portobello mushroom cap on the bottom half of each bun.

3. Spread a generous amount of guacamole over the mushroom cap.

4. Top with a lettuce leaf, a slice of tomato, and a slice of red onion.

5. Place the other half of the bun on top to complete the burger.

Nutritional Information (Per Serving):

- Carbs: 40g

- Fats: 20g

- Fiber: 12g

- Protein: 10g

Eggplant Rollatini with Vegan Pesto

Prep Time: 30 minutes

Cook Time: 40 minutes

Servings: 4

Ingredients:

For the Eggplant Rolls:

- 2 large eggplants, thinly sliced lengthwise

- Olive oil for brushing

- Salt and black pepper to taste

For the Filling:

- 1 cup ricotta cheese (flexitarian option) or vegan ricotta

- ½ cup spinach, chopped

- ¼ cup fresh basil, chopped

- 2 cloves garlic, minced

- Salt and black pepper to taste

For the Vegan Pesto:

- 2 cups fresh basil leaves

- ½ cup pine nuts, toasted

- 2 cloves garlic

- ½ cup nutritional yeast

- ½ cup extra virgin olive oil

- Salt and black pepper to taste
- Juice of 1 lemon

For Assembly:

- 1 cup marinara sauce
- Vegan or regular Parmesan cheese, grated, for topping

Directions:

For the Eggplant Rolls:

1. Preheat the oven to 375°F (190°C).

2. Brush eggplant slices with olive oil, season with salt and black pepper. Bake in the preheated oven for 15 minutes or until they are pliable.

For the Filling:

1. In a bowl, add in the ricotta cheese (or vegan ricotta), chopped spinach, chopped fresh basil, minced garlic, salt, and black pepper. Mix properly.

For the Vegan Pesto:

1. In a food processor, add in the basil leaves, toasted pine nuts, garlic, nutritional yeast, olive oil, salt, black pepper, and lemon juice. Blend until smooth.

For Assembly:

1. Spread a thin layer of marinara sauce on the bottom of a baking dish.

2. Take each baked eggplant slice and spread a spoonful of the ricotta filling on one end. Roll it up and place it seam-side down in the baking dish.

3. Repeat until all the eggplant slices are filled and rolled.

4. Pour the vegan pesto over the eggplant rolls, spreading it evenly.

5. Bake in the preheated oven for 25-30 minutes or until the rolls are heated through.

6. Sprinkle grated vegan or regular Parmesan cheese on top during the last 5 minutes of baking.

Nutritional Information (Per Serving):

- Carbs: 20g
- Fats: 15g
- Fiber: 8g
- Protein: 10g

Quinoa and Black Bean Stuffed Bell Peppers

Prep Time: 20 minutes

Cook Time: 30 minutes

Servings: 4

Ingredients:

- 4 large bell peppers, halved and seeds removed
- 1 cup quinoa, rinsed
- 2 cups vegetable broth
- 1 can (15 ounces) black beans, drained and rinsed
- 1 cup corn kernels (fresh or frozen)
- 1 cup cherry tomatoes, diced
- ½ cup red onion, finely chopped
- 2 cloves garlic, minced
- 1 teaspoon ground cumin
- 1 teaspoon chili powder
- Salt and black pepper to taste
- 1 cup shredded cheddar cheese (flexitarian option) or vegan cheese
- Fresh cilantro, for garnish

Directions:

1. Preheat the oven to 375°F (190°C).

2. In a medium saucepan, add in the quinoa and vegetable broth. Bring to a boil, then reduce heat to low, cover, and simmer for 15 minutes or until quinoa is cooked and liquid is absorbed.

3. In a large mixing bowl, add in the cooked quinoa, black beans, corn kernels, diced cherry tomatoes, chopped red onion, minced garlic, ground cumin, chili powder, salt, and black pepper. Mix properly.

4. Place the bell pepper halves in a baking dish.

5. Spoon the quinoa and black bean mixture into each bell pepper half, pressing down gently to pack the filling.

6. Sprinkle shredded cheddar cheese (or vegan cheese) over the top of each stuffed bell pepper.

7. Cover the baking dish with foil and bake in the preheated oven for 20-25 minutes or until the peppers are tender.

8. Remove the foil and bake for an additional 5 minutes to melt and slightly brown the cheese.

9. Garnish with fresh cilantro before serving.

Nutritional Information (Per Serving):

- Carbs: 45g

- Fats: 10g

- Fiber: 10g

- Protein: 15g

Sweet Potato and Lentil Patties with Avocado Aioli

Prep Time: 25 minutes

Cook Time: 25 minutes

Servings: 4

Ingredients:

For the Patties:

- 2 cups sweet potatoes, peeled and grated

- 1 cup cooked green lentils

- ½ cup breadcrumbs

- ¼ cup red onion, finely chopped

- 2 cloves garlic, minced

- 1 teaspoon ground cumin

- 1 teaspoon paprika

- Salt and black pepper to taste

- 2 tablespoons olive oil (for cooking)

For the Avocado Aioli:

- 1 ripe avocado, peeled and mashed

- ¼ cup mayonnaise (flexitarian option) or vegan mayonnaise

- 1 clove garlic, minced

- 1 tablespoon fresh lemon juice

- Salt and black pepper to taste

Directions:

For the Patties:

1. In a large bowl, add in the grated sweet potatoes, cooked green lentils, breadcrumbs, finely chopped red onion, minced garlic, ground cumin, paprika, salt, and black pepper. Mix properly.

2. Form the mixture into patties, pressing firmly to shape.

3. Heat olive oil in a skillet over medium heat. Cook the patties for 4-5 minutes on each side or until golden brown and cooked through.

For the Avocado Aioli:

1. In a small bowl, add in the mashed avocado, mayonnaise (or vegan mayonnaise), minced garlic, fresh lemon juice, salt, and black pepper. Mix until smooth.

Serving:

1. Serve the sweet potato and lentil patties with a dollop of avocado aioli on top.

Nutritional Information (Per Serving):

- Carbs: 40g

- Fats: 15g

- Fiber: 10g

- Protein: 12g

Coconut Curry Butternut Squash Soup with Quinoa

Prep Time: 20 minutes

Cook Time: 40 minutes

Servings: 6

Ingredients:

- 1 medium butternut squash, peeled, seeded, and diced

- 1 cup quinoa, rinsed

- 1 can (14 ounces) coconut milk

- 1 onion, diced

- 3 cloves garlic, minced

- 1 tablespoon ginger, grated

- 1 tablespoon red curry paste

- 4 cups vegetable broth

- 1 tablespoon olive oil

- Salt and black pepper to taste

- Fresh cilantro, for garnish

Directions:

1. In a large pot, heat olive oil over medium heat. Add diced onion, minced garlic, and grated ginger. Sauté until the onion is translucent.

2. Add diced butternut squash to the pot and cook for 5 minutes, stirring occasionally.

3. Stir in red curry paste and cook for an additional 2 minutes to enhance the flavors.

4. Pour in vegetable broth and bring the mixture to a boil. Reduce heat to simmer and cook until the butternut squash is tender, about 20-25 minutes.

5. While the soup is simmering, cook quinoa according to package instructions. Set aside.

6. Once the butternut squash is tender, use an immersion blender to puree the soup until smooth. Alternatively, transfer the soup to a blender in batches, then return it to the pot.

7. Stir in coconut milk and season the soup with salt and black pepper to taste.

8. To serve, ladle the soup into bowls, top each serving with a spoonful of cooked quinoa, and garnish with fresh cilantro.

Nutritional Information (Per Serving):

- Carbs: 45g

- Fats: 15g

- Fiber: 8g

- Protein: 10g

Spaghetti Squash Alfredo with Broccoli and Sun-Dried Tomatoes

Prep Time: 20 minutes

Cook Time: 40 minutes

Servings: 4

Ingredients:

- 1 medium-sized spaghetti squash, halved and seeds removed
- 1 cup broccoli florets, steamed
- ½ cup sun-dried tomatoes, sliced
- 2 tablespoons olive oil
- 3 cloves garlic, minced
- 1 cup half-and-half (flexitarian option) or plant-based milk
- 1 cup grated Parmesan cheese (flexitarian option) or nutritional yeast
- Salt and black pepper to taste
- Fresh parsley, chopped, for garnish

Directions:

1. Preheat the oven to 400°F (200°C).

2. Place the spaghetti squash halves on a baking sheet, cut side up. Drizzle with 1 tablespoon of olive oil and season with salt and black pepper. Roast in the oven for 35-40 minutes or until the squash is tender. Once cooked, use a fork to scrape out the strands into a bowl and set aside.

3. In a large skillet, heat the remaining 1 tablespoon of olive oil over medium heat. Add minced garlic and sauté until fragrant.

4. Pour in half-and-half (or plant-based milk) and bring to a gentle simmer.

5. Stir in grated Parmesan cheese (or nutritional yeast) and continue to simmer until the sauce thickens.

6. Add the cooked spaghetti squash strands to the skillet, tossing them in the Alfredo sauce until well-coated.

7. Gently fold in steamed broccoli florets and sliced sun-dried tomatoes.

8. Season the dish with additional salt and black pepper to taste.

9. Serve the Spaghetti Squash Alfredo in bowls, garnished with chopped fresh parsley.

Nutritional Information (Per Serving):

- Carbs: 30g

- Fats: 20g

- Fiber: 7g

- Protein: 15g

Portobello Mushroom and Spinach Enchilada Stacks

Prep Time: 30 minutes

Cook Time: 25 minutes

Servings: 4

Ingredients:

- 4 large Portobello mushrooms, stems removed

- 2 cups baby spinach, chopped

- 1 can (15 ounces) black beans, drained and rinsed

- 1 cup corn kernels (fresh or frozen)

- 1 cup enchilada sauce

- 1 cup shredded Monterey Jack cheese (flexitarian option) or vegan cheese

- ½ cup red onion, finely diced

- 2 cloves garlic, minced

- 1 teaspoon ground cumin

- 1 teaspoon chili powder

- 1 tablespoon olive oil

- Salt and black pepper to taste

- Fresh cilantro, for garnish

Directions:

1. Preheat the oven to 375°F (190°C).

2. Place the Portobello mushrooms on a baking sheet, gill side up. Drizzle with olive oil and season with salt and black pepper. Bake in the preheated oven for 15 minutes.

3. In a skillet over medium heat, sauté minced garlic and finely diced red onion until softened.

4. Add chopped baby spinach to the skillet and cook until wilted.

5. Stir in black beans, corn kernels, ground cumin, and chili powder. Cook for an additional 3-4 minutes until heated through. Season with salt and black pepper to taste.

6. Remove Portobello mushrooms from the oven. Spoon the spinach and bean mixture into the center of each mushroom cap.

7. Pour enchilada sauce over each stuffed mushroom cap.

8. Top each mushroom with shredded Monterey Jack cheese (or vegan cheese).

9. Bake in the oven for an additional 10 minutes or until the cheese is melted and bubbly.

10. Garnish with fresh cilantro before serving.

Nutritional Information (Per Serving):

- Carbs: 25g

- Fats: 10g

- Fiber: 7g

- Protein: 15g

Sweet Potato and Chickpea Patties with Cilantro Lime Sauce

Prep Time: 20 minutes
Cook Time: 30 minutes
Servings: 4

Ingredients:

For Patties:

- 2 medium sweet potatoes, peeled and grated

- 1 can (15 ounces) chickpeas, drained and mashed

- 1 cup breadcrumbs

- ½ cup finely chopped red onion

- 2 cloves garlic, minced

- 1 teaspoon ground cumin

- 1 teaspoon smoked paprika

- Salt and pepper to taste

- 2 large eggs, beaten

- Olive oil for cooking

For Cilantro Lime Sauce:

- 1 cup Greek yogurt

- ¼ cup chopped fresh cilantro

- 2 tablespoons lime juice

- Salt to taste

Directions:

1. In a large bowl, add in the grated sweet potatoes, mashed chickpeas, breadcrumbs, red onion, minced garlic, ground cumin, smoked paprika, salt, and pepper. Mix properly.

2. Add beaten eggs to the mixture and stir until everything is evenly combined.

3. Form the mixture into patties, using about ⅓ cup of the mixture for each patty.

4. Heat olive oil in a skillet over medium heat. Cook patties for 4-5 minutes on each side or until golden brown and cooked through.

5. In a small bowl, whisk together Greek yogurt, chopped cilantro, lime juice, and salt to make the cilantro lime sauce.

6. Serve the sweet potato and chickpea patties with a drizzle of cilantro lime sauce.

Nutritional Information (Per Serving):

- **Carbs:** 45g

- **Fats:** 12g

- **Fiber:** 8g

- **Protein:** 10g

Eggplant and Zucchini Noodle Caprese Salad

Prep Time: 15 minutes
Cook Time: 15 minutes
Servings: 4

Ingredients:

- 1 large eggplant, sliced into ½-inch rounds

- 2 medium zucchinis, spiralized into noodles

- 1 pint cherry tomatoes, halved

- 1 cup fresh mozzarella balls, halved

- ¼ cup fresh basil leaves, thinly sliced

- 2 tablespoons balsamic glaze

- 2 tablespoons extra-virgin olive oil

- Salt and pepper to taste

Directions:

1. Preheat the grill or grill pan over medium-high heat.

2. Brush both sides of eggplant slices with olive oil and season with salt and pepper.

3. Grill eggplant slices for about 3-4 minutes on each side, or until tender and grill marks appear. Remove from the grill and let them cool.

4. In a large bowl, add in the zucchini noodles, cherry tomatoes, mozzarella balls, and sliced basil.

5. Dice the grilled eggplant into bite-sized pieces and add it to the bowl.

6. Drizzle balsamic glaze and extra-virgin olive oil over the salad. Toss gently to combine.

7. Season with additional salt and pepper if needed.

8. Serve immediately or refrigerate until ready to serve.

Nutritional Information (Per Serving):

- **Carbs:** 20g

- **Fats:** 15g

- **Fiber:** 6g

- **Protein:** 8g

Chapter 9: 30-Day Meal Plan

Below is a 30-day meal plan to help you successfully begin your flexitarian diet journey. It is important to note that the recipes in this plan can be easily tailored to suit your preferences and dietary requirements. In addition, you can replace any recipe in this meal plan with the wide range of options provided in this cookbook.

Week 1:

Day 1:

Breakfast: Quinoa and Black Bean Fiesta Bowl
Lunch: Sesame Ginger Tofu and Broccoli Stir-Fry
Dinner: Lentil and Spinach Stuffed Shells

Day 2:

Breakfast: BBQ Jackfruit Tacos with Slaw
Lunch: Chickpea and Artichoke Linguine
Dinner: Seared Tempeh "Scallops" with Lemon Butter Sauce

Day 3:

Breakfast: Pesto Zoodle Caprese Salad with Balsamic Drizzle
Lunch: Coconut Curry Tempeh and Vegetable Stir-Fry
Dinner: Portobello Mushroom Cap Burgers with Guacamole

Day 4:

Breakfast: Sweet and Spicy Mango Black Rice Bowl with Crispy Tempeh
Lunch: Walnut and Mushroom Bolognese Spaghetti
Dinner: Teriyaki Glazed Eggplant "Eel" Sushi Bowl

Day 5:

Breakfast: Caprese Style Pesto Quinoa Tacos with Balsamic Reduction
Lunch: Spinach and Ricotta Stuffed Manicotti
Dinner: Cajun Spiced Chickpea Cakes with Remoulade

Day 6:

Breakfast: Thai Basil Coconut Millet Bowl with Crispy Tofu
Lunch: Orange Glazed Cauliflower and Snap Pea Stir-Fry
Dinner: Lemon Dill Quinoa Stuffed Bell Peppers with "Shrimp"

Day 7:

Breakfast: Buffalo Cauliflower and Avocado Tacos
Lunch: Lemon Garlic Edamame and Cherry Tomato Linguine
Dinner: Coconut Curry Butternut Squash Soup with Quinoa

Week 2:

Day 8:

Breakfast: Mediterranean Quinoa and Chickpea Bowl with Tzatziki
Lunch: Miso Glazed Eggplant and Avocado Tacos
Dinner: Artichoke and Hearts of Palm "Crab" Cakes

Day 9:

Breakfast: Edamame and Brown Rice Buddha Bowl
Lunch: Cashew and Vegetable Teriyaki Stir-Fry
Dinner: Blackened Jackfruit "Tuna" Salad Wraps

Day 10:

Breakfast: Mushroom and Walnut Taco Filling
Lunch: Peanut Sauce Quinoa and Edamame Stir-Fry
Dinner: Lemon Herb Grilled Tofu "Fish" Tacos

Day 11:

Breakfast: Roasted Brussels Sprouts and Pomegranate Quinoa Bowl
Lunch: Thai Basil Tempeh and Bell Pepper Stir-Fry
Dinner: Smoked Paprika Seitan "Scallops" with Garlic Aioli

Day 12:

Breakfast: Greek-style Hummus and Falafel Bliss
Lunch: Pineapple Fried Rice with Tofu
Dinner: Spaghetti Squash Pad Thai with Tofu

Day 13:

Breakfast: Sweet Potato and Black Bean Tacos with Chipotle Crema
Lunch: Lemon Garlic Chickpea and Asparagus Stir-Fry
Dinner: Zucchini Lasagna with Cashew Ricotta

Day 14:

Breakfast: Teriyaki Tempeh and Sesame Seed Sensation
Lunch: Hoisin Glazed Portobello Mushroom Stir-Fry
Dinner: Eggplant Rollatini with Vegan Pesto

Week 3:

Day 15:

Breakfast: Tex-Mex Pinto Bean and Corn Salsa Bowl
Lunch: Mango and Cashew Coconut Rice Stir-Fry
Dinner: Portobello Mushroom and Spinach Enchilada Stacks

Day 16:

Breakfast: Pesto Zucchini Noodle and White Bean Bowl
Lunch: Turmeric Roasted Cauliflower and Chickpea Stir-Fry
Dinner: Coconut-Curry Seitan "Shrimp" Stir-Fry

Day 17:

Breakfast: Greek-inspired Chickpea Gyro Tacos
Lunch: Raspberry Teriyaki Tempeh and Snow Pea Stir-Fry
Dinner: Sweet Potato and Lentil Patties with Avocado Aioli

Day 18:

Breakfast: Spicy Chickpea and Roasted Vegetable Delight
Lunch: Mango and Cashew Coconut Rice Stir-Fry
Dinner: Teriyaki Glazed Eggplant "Eel" Sushi Bowl

Day 19:

Breakfast: Lentil and Sweet Potato Harvest Bowl
Lunch: Sesame Orange Glazed Broccoli and Quinoa Stir-Fry
Dinner: Spaghetti Squash Alfredo with Broccoli and Sun-Dried Tomatoes

Day 20:

Breakfast: Cauliflower and Lentil Lettuce Wrap Tacos
Lunch: Lemon Dijon Asparagus and White Bean Linguine
Dinner: Crispy Teriyaki Tempeh "Tuna" Poke Bowl

Day 21:

Breakfast: Caprese Style Pesto Quinoa Tacos with Balsamic Reduction
Lunch: Sesame Ginger Tofu and Broccoli Stir-Fry
Dinner: Spaghetti Squash Alfredo with Broccoli and Sun-Dried Tomatoes

Week 4:

Day 22:

Breakfast: Coconut Curry Tempeh and Vegetable Stir-Fry
Lunch: Lentil and Spinach Stuffed Shells
Dinner: Lemon Herb Grilled Tofu "Fish" Tacos

Day 23:

Breakfast: Thai Basil Coconut Millet Bowl with Crispy Tofu
Lunch: Pineapple Fried Rice with Tofu
Dinner: Cajun Spiced Chickpea Cakes with Remoulade

Day 24:

Breakfast: Roasted Brussels Sprouts and Pomegranate Quinoa Bowl
Lunch: Cashew and Vegetable Teriyaki Stir-Fry
Dinner: Zucchini Lasagna with Cashew Ricotta

Day 25:

Breakfast: Greek-style Hummus and Falafel Bliss
Lunch: Buffalo Cauliflower and Avocado Tacos
Dinner: Teriyaki Glazed Eggplant "Eel" Sushi Bowl

Day 26:

Breakfast: Sweet Potato and Black Bean Tacos with Chipotle Crema
Lunch: Peanut Sauce Quinoa and Edamame Stir-Fry
Dinner: Portobello Mushroom Cap Burgers with Guacamole

Day 27:

Breakfast: Teriyaki Tempeh and Sesame Seed Sensation
Lunch: Raspberry Teriyaki Tempeh and Snow Pea Stir-Fry
Dinner: Sweet Potato and Lentil Patties with Avocado Aioli

Day 28:

Breakfast: Pesto Zucchini Noodle and White Bean Bowl
Lunch: Turmeric Roasted Cauliflower and Chickpea Stir-Fry
Dinner: Artichoke and Hearts of Palm "Crab" Cakes

Day 29:

Breakfast: Greek-inspired Chickpea Gyro Tacos
Lunch: Miso Glazed Eggplant and Avocado Tacos
Dinner: Coconut-Curry Seitan "Shrimp" Stir-Fry

Day 30:

Breakfast: Cauliflower and Lentil Lettuce Wrap Tacos
Lunch: Lemon Dijon Asparagus and White Bean Linguine
Dinner: Crispy Teriyaki Tempeh "Tuna" Poke Bowl

Chapter 10: Dining Out as a Flexitarian

Dining outdoors as a flexitarian can be a delightful and rewarding experience if you know how to navigate it properly. This chapter aims to provide you with practical tips and strategies for making mindful choices when dining out, so that your flexitarian journey can continue to be flavorful and satisfying outside of your kitchen. Learn how to stay true to the flexitarian lifestyle and relish your favorite restaurant meals without compromising.

Exploring Menu Options

When you encounter a wide range of choices on a menu, it's crucial to approach the options with an open and flexible mindset. Here's a guide to assist you in making well-informed choices:

1. Try out Plant-Centric Options: Seek out dishes that revolve around vegetables, legumes, and whole grains. Many restaurants have embraced the trend of including plant-based options on their menus, providing customers with a variety of creative and flavorful choices.

2. Customization is Key: Feel free to customize your order. Consider requesting substitutions such as additional vegetables, tofu, or beans instead of meat. Most restaurants are quite flexible and ready to tailor dishes according to your preferences.

3. Look Out for Flexitarian Buzzwords: Pay attention to words that suggest options suitable for flexitarians. Terms such as "vegetarian," "plant-based," "grilled," and "roasted" are often indicative of dishes that can be easily adjusted to fit the flexitarian style.

4. Alternative Approach: Instead of opting for a conventional main course, you can explore the option of ordering a selection of appetizers or side dishes. This enables you to try out a variety of flavors and guarantees a plant-focused experience.

5. Global Cuisines: Consider trying out global cuisines that typically incorporate plant-based ingredients. Mediterranean, Asian, and Mexican cuisines are known for their wide range of flexitarian-friendly options.

6. Communicate with the Servers: When it comes to communicating your dietary preferences, feel free to share them with the server. They can offer valuable insights into the preparation of dishes and recommend adjustments to accommodate your flexitarian preferences.

Making Smart Dining Choices

Being mindful when eating out as a flexitarian requires a mix of awareness, readiness, and creativity. Here's a helpful guide for navigating menus and making choices that align with your flexitarian goals:

1. Prioritize Vegetables: Opt for dishes which feature a diverse range of vibrant and nutrition-packed vegetables. These dishes usually provide a delightful and rich experience without heavily relying on animal-based ingredients.

2. Lean Protein Selections: Go with lean protein options such as fish, poultry, or plant-based proteins. These choices help you meet your protein requirements while keeping a balance between plant and animal-based foods.

3. Watch Portion Sizes: It's important to be mindful of portion sizes, particularly when it comes to dishes that contain meat. Consider sharing larger portions or choosing appetizer-sized portions to find a good balance.

4. Be Mindful of Cooking Methods: Prioritize grilled, baked, steamed, or roasted dishes over fried or heavily sautéed ones. These cooking methods are less reliant on added fats and preserve the natural flavors of the ingredients.

5. Sauces on the Side: Request sauces and dressings on the side to have better control over how much of it you consume. Doing this also helps you to achieve a more balanced flavor experience.

6. Hydrate with Care: Opt for water, herbal teas, or other low-calorie beverages to go with your meal. This not only promotes hydration but also helps to avoid any unnecessary added sugars or calories.

7. Enjoy Your Treat with Mindfulness: If you choose to indulge, enjoy desserts with your companions at the table or choose smaller portions to fully appreciate the delicious flavors without overdoing it.

By following these tips when dining out, you can enjoy a diverse selection of mouthwatering meals without deviating from your flexitarian lifestyle. The flexibility of the flexitarian lifestyle enables you to embrace and enjoy diverse culinary experiences that support your health and ethical objectives. As you try out different restaurants and cuisines, you'll discover that the world of flexitarian dining is incredibly diverse and offers a wide range of culinary delights

Chapter 11: Maintaining a Healthy and Balanced Flexitarian Lifestyle

Congratulations on adopting the flexitarian lifestyle! As you progress on this journey, the emphasis turns towards maintaining your new approach to eating over the long term. This chapter offers useful information and practical advice to help you integrate a flexitarian lifestyle into your daily routine in a sustainable and fun way. Let's explore the essential aspects of maintaining a healthy and balanced flexitarian lifestyle, including establishing habits for long-term success and creating a flexitarian-friendly environment.

Tips for Long-term Success

1. Gradual Transitions: If you're looking to transition into a flexitarian lifestyle, it may be helpful to make changes gradually. Begin by adding more plant-based meals to your weekly menu and gradually decreasing your consumption of animal products. This methodical approach enhances the chances of achieving long-term success.

2. Variety is Key: Spice up your meals and add variety by trying out a diverse selection of plant-based ingredients, grains, and proteins. Embrace the diverse range of flavors that the flexitarian diet offers, ensuring that monotony doesn't hinder long-term commitment.

3. Meal Planning: Plan your meals in advance to make sure you have a diverse and well-balanced diet. This not only streamlines grocery shopping but also enables you to make mindful choices that support your flexitarian goals.

4. Try Out New Recipes: Continuously broaden your recipe collection by exploring a variety of flexitarian recipes. This cookbook is a great source of inspiration, but don't hesitate to explore other cookbooks, blogs, or cooking classes to add diversity and excitement to your meals.

5. Educate Yourself: Stay well-informed about the nutritional aspects of the flexitarian diet to enhance your knowledge. Gaining a thorough understanding of the nutritional value of various foods enables you to make well-informed decisions that promote your overall health and well-being.

6. Listen to Your Body Cues: Be mindful of how your body reacts to various foods. Every individual has their own distinct nutritional needs, and being attuned to your body's signals can assist you in customizing your flexitarian choices to meet your specific requirements.

7. Flexibility in Social Settings: Being flexible is an important aspect of the flexitarian lifestyle, and it also applies to social situations. When dining out or attending social gatherings, it's important to be flexible and make the most suitable choices without feeling restricted by strict guidelines.

8. Simplify Your Life with Meal Prep: Consider adding meal prep to your routine. Getting your ingredients or meals ready ahead of time can be a real time-saver during busy periods. Plus, it guarantees that you'll always have healthy flexitarian choices at your fingertips.

9. Embrace Whole Foods: Make whole, minimally processed foods a priority in your diet. Whole foods provide exceptional nutritional value and enhance the overall pleasure of a well-rounded diet.

10. Connect with the Community: Join the flexitarian community to connect with like-minded individuals who can provide support, share ideas, and offer motivation. Engaging with online forums, social media groups, or local meet-ups can enhance the sense of community and foster camaraderie, thereby enhancing the overall experience and sustainability of the flexitarian lifestyle.

11. Regular Health Check-ups: Make sure to schedule regular health check-ups to monitor your nutritional status and overall well-being. Seeking guidance from healthcare professionals can help you maintain a diet that meets your needs and make any necessary adjustments.

12. Celebrate Your Progress: Take the time to recognize and appreciate your achievements and milestones as you move forward. Recognizing and appreciating your achievements, whether it's experimenting with a new recipe, handling a difficult dining situation with ease, or making strides towards your health goals, is essential for a positive and long-lasting flexitarian lifestyle.

Remember, the flexitarian lifestyle is all about discovering a harmony that suits your needs. By following these suggestions consistently, you'll have the tools to sustain a healthy and well-rounded flexitarian lifestyle for the long haul.

Chapter 12: Flexitarian Terms Glossary

As you start your flexitarian journey, getting to know important terms and concepts will help you better understand this lifestyle. This glossary offers a thorough introduction to flexitarian terminology, giving you the knowledge to confidently engage in discussions, try out recipes, and explore resources.

1. Flexitarian: A flexitarian is someone who primarily follows a plant-based diet but occasionally includes meat or other animal products in their meals.

2. Plant-based: Describing a diet that mainly focuses on foods derived from plants, including fruits, vegetables, whole grains, legumes, nuts, and seeds. Flexitarians frequently prioritize plant-based options.

3. Whole Foods: Foods that are minimally processed and as close to their natural state as possible. Some examples are fruits, vegetables, whole grains, and legumes. Flexitarians place great emphasis on consuming whole foods due to their richness in nutrients.

4. Plant-Based Protein: Protein sourced from plants, including legumes, tofu, tempeh, and plant-based meat alternatives. Flexitarians include these protein sources in their meals to maintain a well-rounded diet.

5. Meat Alternatives: Products that aim to replicate the taste and texture of meat by utilizing plant-based ingredients. Flexitarians often gravitate towards plant-based meat alternatives like veggie burgers and plant-based sausages.

6. Whole Grains: Grains that preserve their bran, germ, and endosperm, offering a plentiful supply of fiber, vitamins, and minerals. Some examples are quinoa, brown rice, and whole wheat.

7. Legumes: Legumes are a group of plants from the Fabaceae family and it also includes their seeds or fruits. Example of legumes are beans, lentils, and chickpeas. Legumes are highly nutritious and versatile, making them a popular choice in the flexitarian diet.

8. Tofu: A highly adaptable soy-based product known for its subtle taste and varying levels of firmness. Tofu is a popular protein option for flexitarians and can be incorporated into a wide range of delicious savory and sweet recipes.

9. Tempeh: Tempeh is a soy product that has undergone fermentation, resulting in a distinct nutty flavor and a firm texture. It provides a high amount of protein and brings a distinct flavor to flexitarian dishes.

10. Flexitarian Plate: A visual representation showcasing the perfect harmony between plant-based and animal-based foods on a plate. Flexitarians strive for a balanced plate, filling half the plate with vegetables and fruits. A quarter of the plate is allocated to plant-based proteins while the remaining quarter plate is filled with lean animal-based proteins.

11. Ethical Eating: A concept that revolves around making food choices with a focus on ethical considerations, such as sustainability, humane treatment of animals, and environmental impact. Flexitarians frequently take ethical factors into account when making their dietary decisions.

12. Meatless Monday: A worldwide initiative that encourages individuals to forgo meat consumption every Monday, promoting health, sustainability, and ethical eating practices. A significant number of flexitarians incorporate Meatless Monday into their weekly routine.

13. Meal Prep: The process of preparing and packaging meals ahead of time to simplify cooking and guarantee a variety of nutritious, flexitarian-friendly choices for the entire week.

This glossary is a valuable resource to improve your understanding of flexitarian terms, enabling you to fully embrace the flexibility and balance that comes with this lifestyle. As you delve into the wide array of options in the flexitarian cuisine, use this glossary to expand your understanding and make well-informed decisions on your path towards a healthier and more sustainable eating lifestyle.

Conclusion

Congratulations on reading through to the end of this cookbook — *The Complete Flexitarian Cookbook*! We hope this culinary journey has motivated you to adopt the flexitarian approach to eating. The flexitarian lifestyle embraces the benefits of both plant-based and animal-based diets, providing a nourishing and sustainable approach to food that is both delicious and good for your health and the environment.

Within the pages of this cookbook, you've discovered a wide range of delicious and healthy recipes that seamlessly incorporate flexitarianism into your daily routine. The Flexitarian Plate, smart protein choices, and the inclusion of whole grains to your dishes have equipped you with the ability to prepare well-rounded meals that satisfy and nourish.

Keep in mind that the basis of the flexitarian lifestyle is all about being flexible, adaptable, and finding joy in it. Whether you're an experienced flexitarian or new to the lifestyle, the tips for dining out, maintaining a healthy lifestyle, and the glossary of flexitarian terms are valuable resources to help you on your journey.

We highly encourage you to keep exploring, experimenting, and enjoying the diverse world of flexitarian cooking. With a wide range of plant-based options, there are several recipes to choose from. As you step into your kitchen, remember that every meal presents an opportunity to provide your body with nourishment, explore new flavors, and support an ecologically sound food future.

Thank you for joining us on this delightful journey. May your flexitarian lifestyle bring you happiness, good health, and a fresh perspective on the art of mindful and balanced eating. Cheers to a future brimming with delectable, healthy, and meals inspired by flexitarianism!

Index of Recipes

A

Almond Crusted Tofu "Fish" and Chips 87

Artichoke and Hearts of Palm "Crab" Cakes 92

Asian-Inspired Tofu and Broccoli Bowl 15

B

BBQ Jackfruit Tacos with Slaw 27

Blackened Jackfruit "Tuna" Salad Wraps 96

Buffalo Cauliflower and Avocado Tacos 39

Butternut Squash and Sage Farfalle 76

Butternut Squash and Sage Gnocchi with Almond Cream Sauce 83

C

Cajun Spiced Chickpea Cakes with Remoulade 89

Caprese Style Pesto Quinoa Tacos with Balsamic Reduction 45

Cashew and Vegetable Teriyaki Stir-Fry 49

Cauliflower and Chickpea Crust Pizza 107

Cauliflower and Lentil Lettuce Wrap Tacos 32

Chickpea and Artichoke Linguine 67

Cilantro Lime Black Bean and Corn Fusilli 75

Coconut Curry Butternut Squash Soup with Quinoa 116

Coconut Curry Cauliflower "Crab" Soup 102

Coconut Curry Tempeh and Vegetable Stir-Fry 48

Coconut-Curry Seitan "Shrimp" Stir-Fry 94

Crispy Teriyaki Tempeh "Tuna" Poke Bowl 103

E

Edamame and Brown Rice Buddha Bowl 10

Eggplant and Zucchini Noodle Caprese Salad 121

Eggplant Rollatini with Vegan Pesto 112

G

Greek-inspired Chickpea Gyro Tacos 31

Greek-style Hummus and Falafel Bliss 12

H

Harissa Spiced Lentil and Cucumber Yogurt Tacos 42

Hoisin Glazed Portobello Mushroom Stir-Fry 58

J

Jamaican Jerk Cauliflower Tacos with Pineapple Salsa 40

L

Lemon Dijon Asparagus and White Bean Linguine 81

Lemon Dill Quinoa Stuffed Bell Peppers with "Shrimp" 93

Lemon Garlic Chickpea and Asparagus Stir-Fry 57

Lemon Garlic Edamame and Cherry Tomato Linguine 74

Lemon Herb Grilled Tofu "Fish" Tacos 101

Lentil and Spinach Stuffed Shells 66

Lentil and Sweet Potato Harvest Bowl 9

M

Mango and Cashew Coconut Rice Stir-Fry 60

Mediterranean Quinoa and Chickpea Bowl with Tzatziki 19

Mediterranean Stuffed Zucchini with "Feta" and "Shrimp" 97

Mexican-Inspired Cauliflower Rice Bowl 11

Miso Glazed Eggplant and Avocado Tacos 44

Mushroom and Walnut Taco Filling 28

O

Orange Glazed Cauliflower and Snap Pea Stir-Fry 53

P

Peanut Sauce Quinoa and Edamame Stir-Fry 50

Pesto Zoodle Caprese Salad with Balsamic Drizzle 84

Pesto Zoodle Primavera 68

Pesto Zucchini Noodle and White Bean Bowl 14

Pineapple and Quinoa Stuffed Pepper Tacos 37

Pineapple Fried Rice with Tofu 56

Portobello Mushroom and Spinach Enchilada Stacks 119

Portobello Mushroom Cap Burgers with Guacamole 110

Q

Quinoa and Black Bean Fiesta Bowl 7

Quinoa and Black Bean Stuffed Bell Peppers 114

R

Raspberry Teriyaki Tempeh and Snow Pea Stir-Fry 62

Roasted Brussels Sprouts and Pomegranate Quinoa Bowl 24

Roasted Red Pepper and White Bean Penne 71

S

Seared Tempeh "Scallops" with Lemon Butter Sauce 88

Sesame Ginger Tofu and Broccoli Stir-Fry 47

Sesame Orange Glazed Broccoli and Quinoa Stir-Fry 64

Smoked Paprika Seitan "Scallops" with Garlic Aioli 100

Southwestern Corn and Avocado Quinoa Bowl 17

Spaghetti Squash Alfredo with Broccoli and Sun-Dried Tomatoes 118

Spaghetti Squash Pad Thai with Tofu 106

Spicy Chickpea and Roasted Vegetable Delight 8

Spicy Mango Glazed Jackfruit "Shrimp" Lettuce Wraps 98

Spicy Sriracha Eggplant and Tofu Stir-Fry 52

Spinach and Artichoke Stuffed Shells with Walnut Parmesan 79

Spinach and Ricotta Stuffed Manicotti 72

Sundried Tomato and Basil Chickpea Penne 80

Sweet and Spicy Mango Black Rice Bowl with Crispy Tempeh 21

Sweet Potato and Black Bean Tacos with Chipotle Crema 34

Sweet Potato and Chickpea Patties with Cilantro Lime Sauce 120

Sweet Potato and Lentil Patties with Avocado Aioli 115

T

Teriyaki Glazed Eggplant "Eel" Sushi Bowl 91

Teriyaki Portobello Mushroom Tacos 35

Teriyaki Tempeh and Sesame Seed Sensation 18

Tex-Mex Pinto Bean and Corn Salsa Bowl 22

Thai Basil Coconut Millet Bowl with Crispy Tofu 25

Thai Basil Tempeh and Bell Pepper Stir-Fry 55

Tofu and Black Bean Tacos with Avocado Lime Crema 29

Tomato Basil Quinoa Mac 'n' Cheese 77

Turmeric Roasted Cauliflower and Chickpea Stir-Fry 61

W

Walnut and Mushroom Bolognese Spaghetti 70

Z

Zucchini Lasagna with Cashew Ricotta 109

Printed in Great Britain
by Amazon

43017137R00084